CHRISTIAN HEROES

MARY SLESSOR

Forward into Calabar

JANET & GEOFF BENGE

YWAM Publishing is the publishing ministry of Youth With A Mission (YWAM), an international missionary organization of Christians from many denominations dedicated to presenting Jesus Christ to this generation. To this end, YWAM has focused its efforts in three main areas: (1) training and equipping believers for their part in fulfilling the Great Commission (Matthew 28:19), (2) personal evangelism, and (3) mercy ministry (medical and relief work).

For a free catalog of books and materials, call (425) 771-1153 or (800) 922-2143. Visit us online at www.ywampublishing.com.

Mary Slessor: Forward into Calabar

Published by YWAM Publishing
a ministry of Youth With A Mission
P.O. Box 55787, Seattle, WA 98155-0787

ISBN 978-1-57658-148-3 (paperback)
ISBN 978-1-57658-572-6 (e-book)

Eighth printing 2016

Printed in the United States of America

Christian Heroes: Then & Now

Adoniram Judson
Amy Carmichael
Betty Greene
Brother Andrew
Cameron Townsend
Clarence Jones
Corrie ten Boom
Count Zinzendorf
C. S. Lewis
C. T. Studd
David Bussau
David Livingstone
D. L. Moody
Dietrich Bonhoeffer
Elisabeth Elliot
Eric Liddell
Florence Young
Francis Asbury
George Müller
Gladys Aylward
Hudson Taylor
Ida Scudder
Isobel Kuhn
Jacob DeShazer
Jim Elliot
John Flynn
John Wesley
John Williams
Jonathan Goforth
Klaus-Dieter John
Lillian Trasher
Loren Cunningham
Lottie Moon
Mary Slessor
Mildred Cable
Nate Saint
Paul Brand
Rachel Saint
Rowland Bingham
Samuel Zwemer
Sundar Singh
Wilfred Grenfell
William Booth
William Carey

Available in paperback, e-book, and audiobook formats.Unit study curriculum guides are available for select biographies.

www.HeroesThenAndNow.com

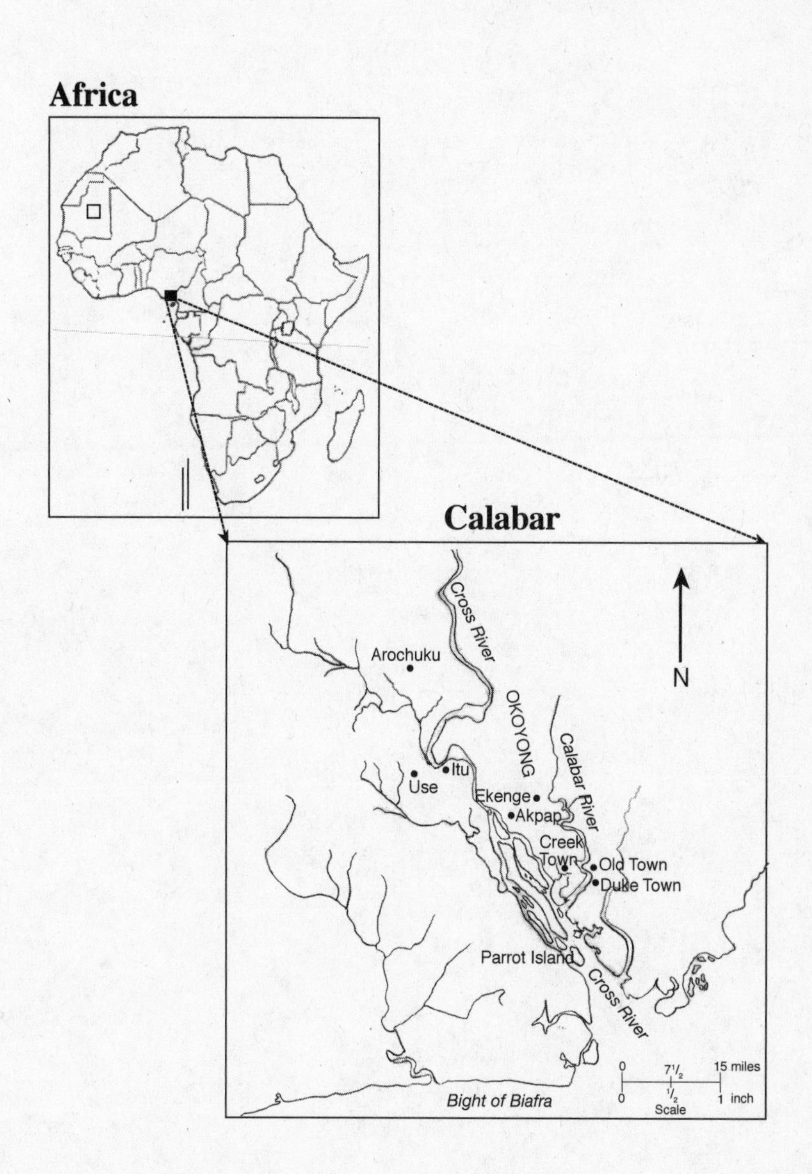
Africa
Calabar
Cross River
Arochuku
N
OKOYONG
Calabar River
Itu
Use
Ekenge
Akpap
Creek
Town
Old Town
Duke Town
Parrot Island
Cross River
0
7 1/2
15 miles
0
1/2
1 inch
Scale
Bight of Biafra

Contents

Chapter 1

The Vice-Consul of Okoyong

The hot West African sun beat down on the clearing at the edge of the village. It was midafternoon, and the court hearing that had started early in the morning was dragging on. Okpono, his near-naked body glistening in the sun, was once again making a spirited argument as to why his brother-in-law should be forced to pay back the money he owed him. The vice-consul of Okoyong sat cross-legged in the shade of a huge kapok tree listening to the argument as she skillfully worked the knitting needles in her hands, passing the woolen yarn over the end of each needle to form a new stitch. The knitting seemed to have a calming effect on her and on the crowd who had gathered to view the proceedings. The vice-consul had already heard Okpono make his argument at least twenty times and listened as Okpono's brother-in-law refuted it each time. She could tell the men were beginning to tire of talking, and soon it would be her turn to take over and render judgment. Experience had taught her that it was important for those involved in the case to talk about it until they could talk no more and were ready to listen to what she had to say.

It amazed Mary Slessor, the blue-eyed, red-haired Scottish woman who served as vice-consul, that she was the one deciding such disputes and that so many people came to observe the proceedings. When Mary first entered the Okoyong region years before, people fled from her in terror. They had never seen a white woman before, and they took her red hair as a sign her head was on fire. But over the years, Mary had won the trust of the people in the region. Now the people called her the "white ma," and instead of fleeing, they flocked around her. No one had done more than the white ma to change the cruel and inhuman customs and practices that had terrorized the people's lives for so many years.

Mary focused her attention on the case. Okpono's brother-in-law was now wrapping up another rebuttal to Okpono's argument, and it was time for Mary to start thinking about rendering judgment. The decision was cut and dried, really, but Mary still had a few things to think on. She was irritated that Okpono would take his brother-in-law to court when he himself neglected his children and took delight in regularly beating his wives, especially the wife who was the sister of the man he had dragged into court. What troubled Mary the most was that the brother-in-law was a hard-working, honorable man who had simply had some bad luck. So while the case was plain and simple—the brother-in-law owed the money and needed to pay it back—Mary was concerned that justice be administered in a broader sense. Besides understanding that debts needed to be repaid, people needed to see that it wasn't okay to neglect their children or beat their wives.

Mary sat knitting in silence, mulling over what to do. After several minutes, she laid aside her knitting and got to her feet. Looking Okpono's brother-in-law squarely in the face she said, "I find you guilty and order you to pay to Okpono the money you owe."

Dejected at losing, the brother-in-law dropped his head. At the same time, a large smirk crept across Okpono's face. But Mary had a surprise for Okpono. She spoke again to the brother-in-law. "I also order you to give Okpono a whipping, right here and now. And be sure you make it hard, or I will fine you for going easy on him."

A look of shock quickly replaced the smirk on Okpono's face. At the same time, looks of satisfaction crept across the faces of those in the crowd. This was justice. The white ma truly understood their ways.

With her duties as vice-consul discharged for the day, Mary gathered up her knitting and placed it into a bag. It was time to eat and then share more of the gospel message with the village. In the morning, Mary would begin the trek back to Ekenge, the village where she lived.

As she sat at the fire that night eating a bowl of corn stew with her fingers, Mary wondered what the people back at the Baxter cotton mill in Dundee, Scotland, would think if they saw her now. They would probably be amazed that she had managed to stay alive for so long in such a harsh environment, especially when so many other missionaries had died within a few years of arriving in Calabar. They might also marvel at the fact that the eleven-year-old girl who had started working at the mill was now vice-consul, the sole administrator of British law in the Okoyong region. Of course, Mary would not have believed it possible back then either, but here she was. There was no denying it—she had grown a lot from being that small girl working at the mill. In fact, she now felt more at home among the people of the Okoyong region than she did among Scottish people in Scotland. Indeed, she now referred to the Africans as "her" people, and they referred to her as *Eka Kpukpru Owo*, the Mother of Us All. It was all a long way from life in Dundee….

Chapter 2

It Was Up to Her

Eleven-year-old Mary Slessor stood by the door of the only house she'd ever known and watched as a neighbor hauled away the kitchen table. The table was being sold to raise money for the family to move to the city of Dundee, Scotland.

"Don't worry about the move, Mary. Things will work out for the best. It will give your father a fresh start," her mother said, patting Mary's bright red curly hair. "There will be new opportunities for you in Dundee. Perhaps you'll even be able to go to school."

Mary's eyes lit up. "That would be wonderful. Do you really think I might get to go?" she asked.

"Once we're all settled in and your father has a steady job, I don't see why not. Now, run along and fold the blankets for me, would you? I've a mind to put them in the bottom of this chest."

Mary skipped happily from the front door of the cottage to the tiny bedroom she shared with her three younger sisters. Her younger brother John slept in the loft above the kitchen. Until a year ago, when he had become weak and died, Robert, her older brother, had slept in the loft as well. With his death, Mary had become the oldest child of Robert and Mary Slessor, after whom the two elder children were named.

As Mary folded the blankets, she thought about what her mother had said and wondered whether things really would be better in Dundee than they were in Gilcomston, near Aberdeen on the northeast coast of Scotland where they lived. Although Mary had never been more than a few miles from her home, her friend Helen had and had told her all about the towns in the lowlands of Scotland. The buildings there were apparently dark and close together, and it was almost impossible to breathe because the thick smoke produced by the factories hung in black clouds above the cities. It sounded horrible to Mary, and not one bit as good as living in Aberdeen, where the wind rustled through the highland heather and down into the city. But surely things in Dundee weren't as bad as Helen said. Otherwise why would her mother be so eager for the family to move there?

Mary knew part of the answer. It was because of her father, a strong, muscular man with curly red hair who told the most exciting stories and whose laugh could fill the whole house. That is, when he was sober. When he was drunk, he turned into a monster. He yelled and screamed and lashed out at his wife and children. And lately he had been drunk more and more. Mary knew it had something to do with his shoemaking business not going well. She had lain awake one night and had heard her mother beg her father to move the family to Dundee, where he could get a steady job in one of the new factories there.

Mrs. Slessor had explained to Mary on several occasions that in this age of machines, the "big" money was to be made in the cities working in the new factories springing up there and not in some backwater community making shoes by hand. It was 1859, and anyone living in Scotland, she insisted, should be taking advantage of the wave of industrialization sweeping across the country.

Mary desperately wanted to believe that moving to Dundee would be a change for the better. She hoped her father would stop drinking and get a job with a regular wage. She also hoped she could attend school. She longed to be able to read and write.

As she finished folding the blankets, Mary heard a commotion outside the cottage and the neighing of a horse. She rushed outside to see the horse and dray that would take them to the ferryboat for the trip down the coast to Dundee.

Two days later, Mary discovered that Dundee was everything Helen had said—and worse. The family was crammed into a dirty two-room apartment on the second floor of a tenement building on Queen Street, right in the heart of one of Dundee's slums. And just as Helen had said, the air was so thick with black smoke that it coated the laundry Mrs. Slessor hung out the window to dry. The laundry was often grimier after it had been washed than before.

Mary helped her mother scrub and clean up the two rooms, but there were two things they could do nothing about. The first was the rats that scurried across the floor of the apartment. It was useless trying to catch them. Hundreds more were living out in the muddy streets ready to move inside and take the place of any rat Mary and her mother managed to kill. The second thing they could do nothing about was the smell, which wafted up through the building from the street below, a mixture of raw sewage and rotting garbage. On warm days, the terrible smell was so overpowering that Mrs. Slessor would keep the windows shut. It was better to endure the heat than open the windows and put up with the foul odor.

Although the family's housing situation was horrible, Mary told herself it didn't matter as long as her father had a job and her mother was happy. And for the first month, that's exactly how things were. Mrs. Slessor busied herself arranging the apartment and taking care of the children while her husband began working for a shoemaker. It was such a relief to Mary to have her father come home at night not smelling of alcohol. Mary was especially delighted when her father began talking about moving the family into a cottage and sending the older children to school. They would do it as soon as he had saved up the money, her father assured everyone.

Regrettably, this change in Mary's father lasted only about a month. One Saturday night, about five weeks after they had moved to Dundee, Robert Slessor came home very late and very drunk. Mrs. Slessor had left his dinner—mutton stew and mashed potatoes—on the table for him. Soon after he arrived home, Mary heard her father throw the plate of food against the wall, cursing because it was as cold as a stone. Tears filled Mary's eyes as she lay still in bed between her sisters. Her stomach ached with hunger as she thought about the biggest chunks of meat that her mother had carefully set aside for her father's plate. Now the food was a splattered mess on the wall, a mess Mary would no doubt have to clean up in the morning.

The shouting went on for a long time, but finally it died down and Mary fell asleep. In the morning she awoke to the sound of her father snoring loudly in the next room. The events of the night before drifted into her mind, and she was glad it was Sunday. At least today she would get to go to church with her mother, brother, and sisters.

Mary liked attending Wishart Memorial Church, especially Sunday school. She enjoyed the stories the pastor told and the missionary reports of the church secretary, who would describe what was happening in Calabar. Mary knew all about Calabar from the missionary stories her mother read to the children from the *Missionary Record,* the missions newsletter of the United Presbyterian Church of Scotland. Calabar was an area in West Africa where, in 1846, just two years before Mary was born, the Presbyterian Church had founded a mission. Mary could even find it on the map, right at the place where the coast of Africa took a sharp bend to the west.

To Mary Slessor, sitting straight and tall in the dark wooden pew Sunday after Sunday, Calabar was everything Dundee was not. It was fascinating and foreign. Mary's big brother Robert had thought so, too, and Mary recalled how together as little children back in Gilcomston they had "played church" together. Robert had always told her, "When I grow up, Mary, I am going to be a missionary, and do you know what? I'm going to take you with me!" Mary had always laughed and replied, "That's a fine plan, Robert, and I'd be glad to be your assistant." Now Robert was dead, but Mary knew that her mother cherished hopes that John would become the missionary of the family. Mary did all she could to fire him with enthusiasm for Calabar.

One Sunday afternoon, as they walked home from church, Mrs. Slessor and Mary fell in step together. The younger children walked on ahead, jumping over the cracks in the sidewalk. Mrs. Slessor spoke quietly. "Mary, I need to talk to you alone.

Let's take the children home and get them something to eat, and then we'll go out walking for a bit. Your father should be awake by now; he can watch the children."

Mary pulled her shawl around her shoulders and tried to imagine what her mother wanted to talk to her about. Her mother sounded so serious, as if she were talking to another adult.

Back at the apartment, Mary held her breath as she waited for her mother to ask her father to watch the children. Her father begrudgingly grunted his agreement, and Mary and her mother slipped outside into the damp afternoon. As they left the building and began walking up Queen Street, Mrs. Slessor began to speak. Her voice was soft, and her eyes were fixed on the cobblestones.

"Mary," she began, "I had such high hopes for us all moving to Dundee. Your father promised me he would stop drinking and get a proper job, but..." she sighed deeply, "after last night it's just not going to happen. He told me he was fired for being rude to the foreman, and I don't think he'll ever hold down a job. Alcohol has got him good and proper."

Mary reached for her mother's hand and held it as they kept walking.

"I've been talking to Mrs. Clunie in the next apartment," Mrs. Slessor went on. "She works in the Baxter cotton mill and says they are hiring women. I'm a good weaver. I'm going to apply for a job tomorrow. I need you to stay home and look after the others," her voice trailed off as she stopped to look her eleven-year-old daughter fully in the face. "Oh, Mary, Mary, lass, I never meant for it to be this way," she sobbed quietly. "I wanted you to go to school and learn. You have a quick mind, and it breaks my heart to see it wasted."

"It's all right, Ma. We'll find a way to cope. I'll go to school one day. It won't be too late," Mary said gently, feeling older than her eleven years. "It's all right, honest."

Mrs. Slessor blew her nose and bent down to kiss her daughter on the cheek. "Whatever else goes wrong," she said, "I will always thank God for giving me a daughter like you, Mary."

A lot more did go wrong in the next few months. Within a few weeks of each other, Mary's two youngest sisters caught diphtheria and died. Secretly, Mary blamed her father for their deaths. If he had been able to keep a job, they would be living in a cottage on the outskirts of town by now instead of being stuck in the middle of Dundee, where the air was foul and the sun never shone between the towering gray buildings.

Despite the death of her sisters, Mary enjoyed being a little mother to the family. The wake-up bell from the mill clanged at five o'clock each morning, and Mary would get up with her mother so they could have a drink of tea together before she left for work. Sometimes her father joined them, but more often than not he was sleeping off a night of heavy drinking.

Things went on this way for about six months until one day in early 1860, when Mary awoke early to hear her mother sobbing quietly into her pillow. Mary crept out into the living room where her parents slept and found her mother in bed alone. She sat down gently on the edge of the bed. "What's wrong?" she quietly asked her mother.

Mrs. Slessor rolled over to look at her daughter and stifled a sob. "I don't have the money for the rent," she said, "and I don't know what to do. Your father found the money I put away under the flour jar for the rent. He spent it all on alcohol. Not that it would have mattered anyway. We would have come to this in the end. The money I make is not enough to keep us all, and your father can't pass a pub without going in and getting drunk." She put her hands over her face. "Oh, Mary, Mary, what are we to do?" she sobbed.

Mary's heart sank. She could see it all very clearly. Her father was away at a pub drunk, and her big brother was dead. It was up to her and her mother to keep the rest of the family together. "I'll get a job," Mary replied. "I won't be able to earn as much as you, but if we put our money together, we should be able to scrape by, don't you think?"

Mrs. Slessor reached out and hugged her daughter. "Mary, I'll make it up to you somehow, you'll see. Here, you must be cold. Come and lie down with me. Your father will just have to stay with the younger children and do his drinking after we get home."

Mary climbed under the thin blanket with her mother.

"There is one good thing," her mother said softly.

"What's that?" asked Mary wearily.

"The mill has just opened a school for the younger workers. Since you're only eleven, they will employ you in the mornings and let you go to school in the afternoon, and then the reverse the next day."

Mary lay in bed, suddenly wide awake. A school! She was going to school! "Oh, Ma," she said, reaching out to hug her mother. "I can stand anything if only I learn to read."

Mary's mother hugged her tightly, and eventually the two of them drifted off to sleep.

The following day, Mrs. Slessor filled two lunch pails, and mother and daughter set off for work together before sunup.

At the mill gate, Mrs. Slessor stopped to talk to another woman, who Mary assumed was some type of supervisor. Mary was right. A minute or two later, her mother beckoned to her. "Mary," she said, turning to her daughter, "this is Mrs. Dugan. Go with her, and she will show you what to do. You will be working this morning, and this afternoon her daughter will take you over to the classroom."

Mrs. Dugan smiled a toothless smile at Mary and beckoned her to follow. They entered a door at the far end of the huge brick building, and a man handed Mary a card with numbers on it. The card was to be used to keep track of the hours she worked.

"Thank you," said Mary.

The man grunted and then said, "Let's see if you're still thanking me when you come out tonight, lassie." He laughed coarsely.

The noise inside the building was deafening. The clanging and banging of machinery echoed inside the largest room Mary had ever seen.

Mrs. Dugan pointed to a cubbyhole where Mary could put her lunch pail. "Leave your shawl and cardigan there, too, lass. It's hot work in here. I'm sure you've been told that already."

Together Mary and Mrs. Dugan walked over to one of the large machines in the room. "Now, I'm only going to explain this to you once," said Mrs. Dugan, "so you'd better listen carefully. You have to be quick to be a piecer. Looks like you're built for it, being so slender."

Mary wiped her brow and tried to concentrate on what the woman was saying. Her head was already swimming. It was so hot in the room. Mary's mother had warned her that the mill owners liked to keep the inside of the mill between eighty and ninety degrees Fahrenheit because they believed it made the quality of the cotton fabric they produced finer, but it was hotter than anything Mary had ever experienced before. Mary took a deep breath. It was going to be hard to work in such heat for hours. Already she found herself longing for lunch time when her mother had told her she would be allowed to sit on a bench outside.

The job of a piecer was simple enough to explain. It took Mrs. Dugan less than five minutes. Basically, Mary had to walk or crawl back and forth between the reels of the spinning machine, tying together the threads on the spinning frames when they broke. The quality of the fabric produced depended on strong threads. The job, however, was much more difficult to perform than it sounded. Most of the time, Mary had to run from one broken thread to another. If she didn't go fast enough, the person operating the machines would clip Mary across the back of the head with her hand. Other times, Mary had to crawl under the machines to reach the bottom threads, coming perilously close to the pulsating machinery. Within an hour or two, she was exhausted and not at all surprised to learn from one of the older girls that a piecer often walked or crawled twenty miles in a day between the spinning machines.

When the lunch whistle blew at noon, Mary picked up her shawl, her cardigan, and her lunch pail and headed out the door, where a rush of cold air greeted her. She struggled to pull her cardigan on. Her fingers throbbed with tiny cuts from the taut threads she'd had to tie, and her feet were so tired that every step was an effort. She slumped onto a wooden bench and rested her back against the rough bricks of the mill wall. Overhead, thick black smoke belched into the air. Other workers talked and joked with each other, but Mary was too tired to join in.

Once she had eaten her bread and suet, Mary went to find Mrs. Dugan, who was sitting in the midst of a group of older women laughing raucously at a joke. Mary waited politely for Mrs. Dugan to notice her. Finally the woman did. "Luv, now, how did your first day go?" Mrs. Dugan asked kindly.

Mary smiled. "Fine, thank you," she replied, glad her first day of work was over.

"I suppose you'll be wanting Janet to show you where the classroom is. Just a minute. I'll call her." Without moving from where she was sitting, Mrs. Dugan yelled over the surrounding din. "Janet, get over here. I've got a new lass for you to meet."

Mary watched as a tall, dark-haired girl walked over to them.

Half an hour later, Mary was sitting in a chair staring at a chalkboard. The room was long and narrow, and the lighting was so poor that Mary had to squint to see what the teacher was writing. The teacher was explaining the schedule for the week which included reading, writing, arithmetic, singing, sewing, knitting, and geography. Mary's eyes sparkled as she listened. She could stand working half days in the hot, sweaty mill as long as she got to go to school for the other half of the day. If she walked home exhausted every evening, it didn't matter. She was learning to read and write, and that made everything worth it.

Chapter 3

Tragedy and Drudgery

It was a dismal, damp Sunday afternoon not long after Mary had started working at the mill. It was her one day a week off, and she spent the afternoon walking with three other girls from her tenement building. As they strolled along past a house at the bottom of King Street, an old woman came out to greet them. Mary recognized her from church. "Hello, girls," the woman said. Then peering at Mary, she asked, "Aren't you the young Slessor girl who goes to Wishart Memorial Church?"

"Yes, ma'am," replied Mary.

"Well, why don't you come in for a while and bring your friends with you. You all look so cold. I have a fire going, and I just pulled a fresh batch of scones from the oven. How does that sound to you?"

Mary looked at the other girls. She knew they were probably no more interested in visiting with the old woman than she was. Yet a warm fire and fresh scones were hard to pass up. "Well, we can come in, but just for a moment," Mary finally agreed. "My mother will be expecting me home soon."

A glowing, hot fire crackled in the fireplace, and the four girls were soon crowded around it, eating scones and drinking hot, sweet tea. The old woman asked Mary what she had learned in Sunday school that morning, and Mary told her. Then the old woman bent down and poked the fire with a stick. The fire flared up, and sparks shot up the chimney. Abruptly, the woman sat back in her chair and changed the conversation. She looked right at Mary and said, "You know, lassie, if you were to put your hand in that fire, it would sear it completely, and you would be in terrible pain."

Mary nodded politely, wondering whether the old woman was a little crazy. Before she could decide, the old woman went on. "The Bible tells us that hell is like that fire. It burns forever and ever, and those who don't accept the Lord Jesus Christ will spend their eternity there. Their bodies will be seared, their throats parched, but there will be no way out and no end to it. Do you want to burn in hell, lassie?"

Mary shook her head. Given the old woman's description, who in her right mind would want to burn in hell? At the same time, Mary felt an unexpected sense of dread overcome her. She became terrified she'd end up in hell and never see Robert and her sisters again.

"Well, you need to repent of your sins and ask the good Lord to forgive you," the old woman continued. "Do you want to do that?"

Mary nodded, forgetting that her friends were in the room. All she could see was the bright orange glow of fire. "I would," she finally said, meaning it.

The old woman led Mary through a simple prayer, and soon afterwards the girls left her house. As they walked back to their tenement building in the rain, they were all too embarrassed to mention what the old woman had said.

Much to her surprise, lying in bed that night Mary felt more peaceful than she could ever remember. It had been the thought of hell that had convinced her to pray, and now she had no fear of ending up there. But she felt something else, too. She had a wonderful feeling that God was watching over her and somehow things would work out for her.

The next Sunday, Mary told the Sunday school superintendent she had prayed to accept Jesus Christ into her heart and asked if there was some way she could be useful at church. The superintendent suggested she assist by teaching a Sunday school class for the younger children, an assignment Mary accepted with great enthusiasm.

Being a Christian made Mary glad for all she was learning in school at the mill. Mary was soon able to read passages from the Bible as well as storybooks.

She especially liked to read missionary stories. And more than anything, she loved to read about David Livingstone, the missionary explorer in southern Africa. The more she read about Livingstone, the more she found herself identifying with him. They had much in common. David Livingstone was from Scotland, he was the second child in a family with seven children, and like Mary, he had worked in the cotton mills as a boy. But there were some big differences, too. David Livingstone was a man, and men got to lead much more adventurous lives than women. Livingstone was also a brilliant person who had studied and become a doctor so that he would have a practical skill to offer the natives in Africa. Mary had no skills anyone would want. True, she could tie threads on a weaving machine, but that was a skill that was not likely to be useful on the mission field.

Mary sighed as she read about David Livingstone. Their lives may have started out similarly, but she would never be able to do what Livingstone had done. Mary was a woman, and women didn't do such things. So instead, Mary read about David Livingstone to her brother John, who was now also a Christian and eager to become a missionary when he grew up. Secretly, Mary hoped that one day she might be his assistant, as she had promised to be Robert's before he died. Yet everything about her drab life told her it was a far-fetched dream. The family needed her wages so they could all eat, and if Mary followed the course of those women around her, she would work in the mills until she was either too old or too sick to work any longer.

When Mary was fourteen years old, she was allowed to operate a loom. She was now too old to go to the mill school for half-time school, but she did attend evening classes. This meant that she worked from six in the morning until six at night and then went to school for two hours before returning home. The night school teacher was impatient and had little time for tired students. If one of the students could not follow the work on the blackboard, the student would be made to stand for the remainder of the class in order to stay awake. This had happened to Mary on several occasions when she had been extra tired as a result of being awakened the night before by her father's terrifying, drunken ravings.

The new loom job also meant that Mary was paid a few pennies more each week and could sit down to work instead of running or crawling for twelve hours a day. It was a good thing the job paid more, because in 1862, Mrs. Slessor was expecting another baby. This news was not a happy prospect. It meant that fourteen-year-old Mary would be the only steady source of income for the family while her mother took time off with the new baby. Later in the year, baby Janie was born. She was a particularly small, delicate baby, and no one expected her to survive more than a few months.

Mary worked harder than ever at the mill. Her aim was to get a promotion to one of the big new power looms, where the weavers were paid more than anyone else in the mill. As each day wore on and the shuttle flew back and forth across the loom in rhythmic monotony, Mary would pray for missionaries or plan in her head what she would teach to her Sunday school class.

Around this time, in the heart of the worst slum in Dundee, Wishart Memorial Church made plans to begin classes teaching children to read and write and learn about the Bible. Mary asked the Sunday school superintendent if she could become one of the teachers. At first he refused. Mary was petite, and the superintendent told her he was worried something bad might happen to her. After all, the roughest gangs in Dundee roamed the area and had already let the church know it would not be welcome in "their" territory.

Mary insisted she could do the job, and eventually the superintendent relented and allowed her to try it for a while. Mary had to promise, however, never to venture alone into the Pends, as the slum was called. She was to have one of the church elders with her at all times for protection. Mary agreed to this and delighted in her new teaching responsibilities. This new opportunity became all that kept her going through the long, dreary days at the mill.

It didn't take long for the gangs to show themselves. In the third week, Mary decided to go to the classroom early. She needed to write a lesson on the chalkboard before the students arrived, but she had forgotten all about her promise never to go into the Pends alone. As she turned the key in the classroom lock, she was aware of someone standing close behind her. She swung around to see four teenage boys leering at her.

"So, Carrots, you're going in to teach the Bible, are you?" one of the boys said, reaching out to pull her red hair.

"Yes, I am," Mary replied firmly, swinging her head away. "Would you like to come in?" she asked, her heart beating wildly.

The biggest boy laughed. "Nay. But we'd like to have a bit of fun with you though. Hold her arms, lads," he commanded.

Two of the other boys grabbed Mary's arms, and although she struggled, Mary couldn't escape their strong grip.

"Now, let's see how you like this," said the lead boy, taking a string from his pocket. Tied onto the end of the string was a piece of heavy metal with razor-sharp edges. "Tell me you'll go home and forget this foolishness, and I'll let you go. Otherwise we'll see how brave you really are."

Mary stared up at the piece of metal and then at the boy. Her blue eyes opened wide with fear and defiance. "Do what you want to me, but you'll not get me to give up my Bible teaching," she said, waiting to see what would happen next.

The lead boy held the string above Mary's head and swung the razor-sharp piece of metal back and forth, letting it get closer to Mary's face with each swing.

"Are you ready to give up yet?" taunted the boy on her left.

Mary didn't say a word. The metal was only a quarter of an inch from her forehead now. A few more swings and it would hit her.

"This is how the Chinese torture people," goaded the third boy, as the sharp piece of metal gouged a cut across Mary's forehead. Blood flowed down her face, but Mary kept her eyes open and stared directly at her tormentor.

Suddenly, the boy stopped swinging the piece of metal. "That's enough," he said briskly and then added, "She's tough, boys."

The other boys released Mary's arms. Mary reached for the handkerchief in her pocket and pressed it against her wound.

"Now you've had your fun, won't you come in and see what this is all about?" Mary invited with a smile.

Whether it was because she was talking to them instead of screaming with fear, Mary did not know, but whatever the reason, the boys meekly followed her inside. Soon they were joined by twenty or so other children and teenagers, and before the day was over, the boy who'd tormented Mary with the piece of metal had become a Christian.

Mary often smiled when she thought about the incident. She was not the bravest person in the world, but the bullies at the door that day had taught her one thing: They had wanted her to be scared, and when she wasn't, they had given up. It was a lesson she would not forget.

Though things were going well for Mary, tragedy struck the family again. This time it was Mary's father, who developed a bad cough that turned into pneumonia, from which he quickly died. Mary felt many different emotions at his funeral. On the one hand, she was sad; she would miss him. When he was sober, he had been a kind father. On the other hand, when he was drunk, he had seemed like a cruel stranger who stole money from the family and spent it on alcohol, and Mary was relieved that there would be no more of his drunken rages at home. Her father's funeral also made life seem short and very fragile to Mary. Of the six members of the Slessor family who had moved to Dundee four years before, only three were now alive. Still, life in Dundee was no better or worse for the Slessors than it was for the thousands of other families who had moved to the city in search of something better and instead found only tragedy and drudgery.

Mary's skill at operating her weaving loom continued to improve until she was given two sixty-two-inch wide looms to run at the same time. This required a great deal of speed and coordination on her part, and although she was exhausted at the end of each day, she was thankful for the extra money she earned operating the two looms. Year after year, Mary's looms turned out a variety of cotton fabrics: canvas for ships' sails, cotton sheets, tablecloths, flour sacks, even dish towels for Queen Victoria's palace in London.

When Mary was twenty-five years old, her brother John contracted tuberculosis. John's doctor advised a change of climate as quickly as possible. All the family's money was pooled and the furniture was pawned to cover the cost of a ticket to send John to New Zealand to recuperate. Mrs. Slessor and Mary and her two sisters prayed each night that John would make a full recovery and soon return to Scotland to train as a missionary. But it was not to be. A week after arriving in New Zealand, John died, half a world away from his mother and sisters.

While John's death was a bitter blow to Mary, Mary's mother was particularly depressed about it. Now both her sons were dead, and there would be no one bearing the Slessor name to carry the gospel message to foreign lands. There would be no missionary to make her proud. Or so she thought.

Chapter 4

A Post of Honor

With shaking hands, Mary untied her purse strings and pulled out a penny, which she handed to the newsboy waiting outside the mill. The newsboy took the penny and handed Mary a newspaper, which she carefully folded in half and tucked under her arm. As Mary made her way home for the night along the narrow cobbled streets, her sisters Susan and Janie, who also now worked at the mill, walked up behind her. They had seen the newspaper headline, too, and the three sisters walked home in silence. The front page headline echoed in Mary's head as she walked: "Livingstone's Body Arrives in Southampton."

Mary wearily climbed the stairs and opened the door to their dingy apartment. Her mother was stirring a pot of boiling vegetable soup on the gas stove in the kitchen. "What's the matter, lass?" she asked when she saw the look on Mary's face.

Mary said nothing. Instead she took the newspaper from under her arm and spread it on the table. Her mother wiped her hands on her apron and peered at it. "I'm so sorry. To think such a wonderful man has left us. God bless him, and all who follow him," she said, placing her arm lovingly around Mary's shoulders.

Mary adjusted the lamp and sat down to carefully read the text of the news story. "So, it was all true," she finally said when she'd finished reading. "It was Livingstone's body after all. They're going to bury him in Westminster Abbey."

For the past seven or eight years, there had been rumors that David Livingstone was dead or dying. The year before, in May 1873, a fresh rumor surfaced indicating he had died in a native hut in the heart of Africa. It was hard to know whether this was true or not. Even when a body was carried to Zanzibar by two natives who claimed it was the body of David Livingstone, it was difficult to say whether it really was or whether it was the body of some other white man. However, as the paper spread in front of Mary confirmed, the body was without a doubt that of David Livingstone. A famous surgeon in London had examined it and found the fracture in the left arm from an incident in which Livingstone had been mauled by a lion.

"It says he died inland on the banks of the Molilamo River, still looking for the source of the

Nile. His servants buried his heart under a tree right where he died and embalmed his body. Then it says...." Mary ran her finger across the text to find her place. "It says, 'The faithful servants Susi and Chuma then carried the body of their honored master many hundreds of miles to the coast so it could be transported back for burial in his beloved homeland.'" Mary shook her head. "They must have loved him a great deal to go to all that trouble," she said.

Later that night as Mary lay in bed, she thought about David Livingstone and all his brave adventures. Then she remembered his famous words, "I don't care where we go as long as we go forward." *Go forward,* Mary thought to herself. *I'm not going forward. I'm not going anywhere. I'm twenty-seven years old, I work in a cotton mill twelve hours a day, six days a week, and the little spare time I have I spend helping out at church. But that's not enough. There has to be more to life for me.* She rolled over and prayed, "God, I want to go forward like David Livingstone. Send me somewhere, anywhere. Just send me out to be a missionary."

When Mary arose at five o'clock the next morning, her mind was remarkably clear, so clear, in fact, she wondered why she hadn't thought of it earlier. Of course. God wanted *her* to be the missionary in the family. Robert and John couldn't go now. They were both dead, but she could go alone. Her two sisters were old enough to look after her mother. Two mill wages were ample to keep three people. Besides, Mary told herself, if she lived frugally on the mission field, she might even be able to send a little money home to help support her mother.

It took Mary a long time to gather the courage to tell her mother of her plan. Mrs. Slessor had been dependent on Mary for many years now, and it wasn't going to be easy for her to accept her daughter's leaving. Days slipped by without Mary's saying anything, until Mary finally realized that if she didn't tell her mother soon, her dream of being a missionary would start to fade and she would end up spending the rest of her life weaving fabric in a cotton mill in Dundee, Scotland.

"Mother," Mary began after lunch one Sunday, "I want to apply to the Foreign Missions Board to go overseas and take the gospel message to the heathen, just like David Livingstone. I've thought about this for a long time, and I think you and Janie and Susan can all manage without me." She held her breath and waited for her mother's reaction.

"I couldn't be more proud, lassie," said Mrs. Slessor, getting up from her chair and rushing over to hug her daughter. "To think I'll be reading about a 'Missionary Slessor' in the *Missionary Record* after all!"

"But I hate to leave you," replied Mary, a little taken aback by her mother's unexpected enthusiasm.

"And a part of me will hate to see you go, Mary. But I'd never enjoy another day with you if I thought you'd stayed home instead of answering God's call just because of me. Susan and Janie can look after me well enough. You be sure to write now."

"You talk as if I'm leaving tomorrow," laughed Mary with relief. "There's a lot of hurdles to overcome. First, I have to get accepted by the missions board. I have only two years of schooling. David Livingstone was a doctor and an ordained minister when he became a missionary. I'm a far cry from that!"

"That's true," replied her mother, "but you have made the most of the opportunities you've had. Hardly any of the mill girls can read a word, and there you are reading English literature in your spare time. And not only that, but you've done so well with the Sunday school."

"I suppose you're right," said Mary, shrugging her shoulders. "I know I could never run a mission station or anything that grand, but I would be a good assistant to someone…." Her voice trailed off, and as her eyes met her mother's, Mary knew they were both thinking about Robert and John.

"Where do you think you'll go? There are so many places where the church is working," inquired her mother.

"I don't know. I don't have any special skills, so I'll go wherever I'm sent," Mary answered.

The United Presbyterian Church of Scotland had missionaries working in India, China, Japan, and Africa. In her heart, Mary really wanted to go to Calabar on the west coast of Africa. However, she thought she had a better chance of being accepted as a missionary if she didn't name a specific mission field were she wanted to serve. With no real skills, she would consider herself blessed to be posted anywhere.

Finally, in the winter of 1875, after completing mountains of paperwork, Mary was called to an interview with the local division of the Foreign Missions Board. The board members had read her application and now wanted to talk with her in person.

Mary knocked on the large ornately carved door at the side of Wishart Memorial Church and waited. She chided herself for feeling so nervous. After all, she knew many of the people on the board—one of them was her good friend, James Logie. Still, this was one of the most important days of her life, and she wanted everything to go right. Today she would find out whether there was a place for a twenty-eight-year-old weaver on the mission field and, if there was, where it would be.

The sturdy door swung open, and Mary was invited into a large wood-paneled room where seven men sat around an oval table. James Logie greeted her and invited her to sit down. Mary was glad to sit—her knees were knocking and her legs wobbling.

"Now, Miss Slessor, we have considered your application carefully," began one of the church elders, an older, balding man whom Mary did not know well.

Mary held her breath, her heart thumping loudly in her chest.

"As it happens," the elder went on, "we have a

need for a teacher in Calabar. Would you be interested in going there?"

"Calabar?" Mary let out a gasp. They wanted to send her to Calabar! She could hardly believe it! For a moment she forgot to answer the question. Then she remembered where she was. "Oh, yes! I would love to go to Calabar. I can't think of anywhere I would rather be!" she exclaimed. "When can I go?"

The church elder smiled at her. "It's good to see such enthusiasm, but it's a hard place we're sending you to, remember that. Several of the other board members had some doubts about your going." He paused for effect before going on. "After all, you're a tiny lass. Africa is a hard mission field, and Calabar is the hardest of all. Still, you have proved yourself with your Sunday school work."

"Thank you, thank you," replied Mary. "I won't let you down."

The meeting lasted several more minutes, and Mary had many questions, though only a few of them could be answered right then. The committee recommended that Mary go to Edinburgh for three months of formal teacher training and plan on sailing for Africa in the late summer of 1876. A veteran Scottish missionary couple, Mr. and Mrs. Thomson, would be returning to Nigeria at that time, and it would be good if Mary could sail on the same ship with them.

"I'll be in touch with you soon," said James Logie, patting Mary on the arm as he showed her to the door. "There's a lot of planning to be done, but we're here to help you. Congratulations. You'll make a grand missionary, I'm sure of that."

Mary walked home in a daze. She had spent so much time preparing herself for being rejected that she could hardly absorb the reality of what had happened. The words of James Logie kept playing in her mind, "You'll make a grand missionary, I'm sure of that." Mary wasn't so sure, but she would try her hardest. God had something for her to do in Calabar. In truth, Mary had no inkling that day of what lay ahead of her, the adventures she would have, the dangers she would face, and the fame that would follow her.

Mrs. Slessor was thrilled to hear that Mary had been accepted and, along with Susan and Janie, did whatever she could to help Mary prepare. She and Mary scanned past copies of the *Missionary Record* to see whether there was any information they had overlooked about Calabar, even though Mary had read the newsletters so many times she virtually knew them by heart. One issue of the newsletter in particular fascinated her. It contained a history of the mission in Calabar. The Calabar mission had been started thirty years before in Duke Town by the Reverend Hope Waddell. Its purpose was to have missionaries work among a group of natives who had originally been shipped off to Jamaica as slaves. Jamaica was a British colony, and when slavery was outlawed in all British territories in 1807, the slaves were set free. Many of them wanted to return to their homeland. As a result, a large group of ex-slaves had settled in Calabar, and missionaries had been sent out to Africa to work among them.

Mary was fascinated to think that after reading about the mission for so many years she was finally going to see it for herself. She might even get to meet the children of some of those ex-slaves. It all sounded so exotic. She had tried many times before to imagine the missionary compound on Mission Hill above Duke Town. She knew the names of the four other small towns dotted up the Calabar River: Old Town, Creek Town, Eknetu, and farthest inland, Okofiorong. Each of these five towns had its own mission station led by an ordained Presbyterian minister assisted by two or three schoolteachers.

Mary was assigned to work at the original mission site in Duke Town under the guidance of the Reverend and Mrs. Anderson. She had heard the Andersons speak at a missionary meeting several years before. Of course, she had no idea then that she would be one of their teaching assistants. If she had, she would have asked them a million questions! Still, it was comforting to have some idea of the people she was going to be living with.

Soon December arrived, time for Mary to begin her teacher training in Edinburgh. She found leaving difficult, even though she would be back in Dundee to say good-bye before leaving for Africa. Mary loved everything about Edinburgh. Huge Edinburgh Castle, the ancient home of Scottish kings, sat atop Castle Rock. Each day Mary stared up at its imposing stone wall and eight-hundred-year-old turrets as she walked along Princess Street on her way to Canongate Normal School, where she was paired with a qualified teacher. Mary diligently took notes on how to teach children to read and write and how to manage a classroom. It wasn't long before she herself was teaching the class, with the other teacher giving her helpful hints and advice.

Advice on teaching wasn't the only kind of advice Mary got in Edinburgh. Many members at Edinburgh's Bristo Street Presbyterian Church gave her advice concerning Calabar. Some in the congregation thought it was a foolish idea for her to go there. Hadn't she heard that Africa was known as the white man's grave? Didn't she know that only one in every five missionaries lasted the first four years on the mission field? Didn't she know that wild animals lurked along pathways, mysterious diseases struck people dead overnight, and natives dressed in wild costumes roamed the jungle, killing at will? Mary did know, but it did not deter her one bit. It almost seemed to have the opposite effect. Mary became more convinced than ever that she should be going to Calabar. When one friend begged her not to go, pointing out that she would probably not survive her first year in Africa, Mary replied, "Calabar is a post of honor. Since few missionaries volunteer for that section, I wish to go because my Master needs me there the most."

Not only was Mary able to brush off warnings about her plans, but she was so enthusiastic that two of her new friends, both of whom also happened to be named Mary, were inspired to volunteer as missionaries! They were both offered posts in China. Together, the three women visited various churches in and around Edinburgh, speaking about the need for missionaries. They were soon dubbed the "Three Marys," and they were enormously popular wherever they spoke. Mary herself did as little speaking as possible, however, leaving the other two to explain their missionary callings.

After Mary had spent twenty weeks at Canongate Normal School, the senior teacher was convinced that Mary had become a well-trained teacher and that it was time for her to return to Dundee and say good-bye to her family.

Since leaving her mother was of great concern to her, Mary was pleased to find her mother and her sisters all well and in good spirits when she returned. Sixteen-year-old Janie and twenty-six-year-old Susan had done a good job of taking care of each other and their mother. Mary spent three whirlwind weeks in Dundee, packing her trunks with her new "missionary uniform"—starched white blouse, dark woolen skirt, and sun hat—speaking at nearby churches when she could not avoid it, and squeezing in as much time as possible with her family.

Finally, the morning of July 30, 1876, arrived. It was a day Mary had both longed for and dreaded. Today she would say good-bye to her simple, predictable life in Scotland. Many people turned out at the train station to see her off. As the train lurched forward, Mary pulled down the window and waved.

"Pray for me," she wailed until the platform disappeared from sight and with it nearly everyone she'd ever loved.

Chapter 5

On African Soil

Mary peered out the coach window. She was getting close to her destination, the Liverpool docks. She could see the tall masts of ships rising above the warehouse roofs. Her heart beat faster as the coach rounded a final bend and the horses came to a stop.

"Well, here we are, and right on time," commented one of two men from the Foreign Missions Board who had escorted her to Liverpool. He snapped his pocket watch shut and slipped it back into his vest pocket. "How are you doing, Mary?" he asked.

Mary didn't know how to answer the question simply. She had so many thoughts and emotions swirling inside her. She was excited to be in the midst of such a bustling scene. Through the window she could see sailors, merchants, stevedores, and other assorted people. Her gaze fell upon the steamer *Ethiopia,* with its tall masts and smokestacks. The ship would carry her away from Britain and across a vast stretch of ocean to a place where malaria, yellow fever, and blackwater fever ran rampant, claiming the lives of many foreigners. The idea both exhilarated and frightened Mary. "God, guide me and use me as You will," she silently prayed as she climbed down from the coach.

An hour later, her belongings were safely stowed in her tiny cabin and Mary had been introduced to the captain and Mr. and Mrs. Thomson. On deck, she stood and watched as the last of the cargo, including some huge kegs, was hoisted aboard and lowered into the hold.

Finally, at 3:15 P.M., August 5, 1876, Mary Slessor felt the large steam engine in the bowels of the ship begin to vibrate under her feet. The gangway was slowly lowered onto the dock. "Cast off forward, cast off aft," yelled the captain.

Mary watched as the ropes that bound the ship to the dock were released. Within a minute or two, the *Ethiopia* was floating freely. Suddenly the water at the stern began to froth like boiling water as the ship edged away from the dock. A loud cheer went up from the people ashore as they bid farewell to the passengers aboard. As the *Ethiopia* steamed away down the Mersey River, the noise of the busy dockyard slowly faded in the distance.

Within an hour, the bow of the ship was bobbing in the turbulent waters of the Irish Sea. Mary soon began to feel seasick. She excused herself from dinner and went to lie down in her cabin. She unlatched her bunk and folded it down, leaving scarcely enough room in the cabin for her to undress.

Mary found it was much more difficult to rest than she had imagined it would be. The ship pitched up and down and rolled from side to side. She was glad she hadn't eaten any dinner. Finally, sometime after midnight, she fell into a fitful sleep.

The following morning Mary felt more seasick than ever. She couldn't bear to get out of bed. Mrs. Thomson visited her several times during the day, bringing her tea and rolls. It took three days for Mary to finally get her "sea stomach" and venture back up on deck.

The ship by then had long since passed Land's End and was now in the open waters of the North Atlantic. The sails billowed overhead in the brisk southerly wind. The steam engine the captain had used to maneuver the ship out of Liverpool harbor was now silent. Mary wondered whether something was wrong with the engine, but at breakfast she learned it was fine. The steamer did not carry enough coal to run the engine for the entire trip. Instead, the ship was fully rigged with sails, which were used to move the ship along in the open sea. The engine was used for maneuvering in and out of port, in emergencies, and when the ship was fighting a strong head wind or current.

As Mary stood on deck that morning looking out across the steely gray ocean, she was filled with excitement as the reality of the moment swept over her. She was finally on her way to be a missionary. The next land she would see would be Africa!

The ship sliced through the ocean at ten knots. Mary passed much of the time with Mr. and Mrs. Thomson, who were returning to the Cameroon Mountains in West Africa to build and run a home for missionaries who needed care and rest during bouts of illness. The Thomsons would be disembarking with Mary at Duke Town and traveling on to their final destination from there. Mr. Thomson had visited the Calabar region several times before and was able to give Mary some idea of what she might face. It all sounded so unreal to Mary, like something from an adventure novel.

Dr. Thomson explained that there were many tribes in the area. The tribe that inhabited the coast of Calabar was called the Efiks. In the past, the Efiks had been the group who dealt with the slave traders. Now they dealt with European traders who came to buy palm oil to ship back to England. Since this was the first time Mary had heard of palm oil, one night at dinner she asked Mr. Thomson what it was used for.

"Well," Mr. Thomson replied, "it has a surprising number of uses. It makes wonderful oil for machines, and the purer grades can also be used for cooking, making candles, and making soap."

"And the Efiks are the ones who trade this?" Mary asked.

"Yes," said Mr. Thomson. "They're the middlemen. The other tribes bring them their oil, and they arrange to sell it, or if the trader is looking for high-quality oil, they will sell him the palm nuts to be shipped back to England for processing. The Efiks make a handsome profit, I might add."

"And how do we pay them? Is it in English pounds?" asked Mary, wanting to know as much as she could about Calabar.

Mr. Thomson shook his head. "No, not pounds," he said sadly. "English money is of no interest to the Efiks. There's a currency in Africa that is much more valuable than money…." He paused for a moment and then continued. "Alcohol. This ship is loaded down with rum and gin. That's what the captain will use to trade with the coastal tribes for palm oil."

Mary's heart sank. She remembered seeing the kegs being rolled down into the holds back in Liverpool, though she had no idea what was in them. She thought back to her father. She knew exactly what alcohol could do to a person and the person's family, friends, and community. When she'd thought of Africa, she hadn't imagined for a moment that her own country would use alcohol as a means of payment. She was disappointed and saddened at the thought of this type of trade.

"And what about the people the Efik trade with, the inland tribes?" Mary asked.

Mr. Thomson took a slice of bread and placed it on his side plate, then pointed to the bread with his knife. "You know, Mary," he said, "Africa is a lot like this piece of bread. It has a thin crust around the outside. Europeans have been all around the outer edge of Africa. The coast is well mapped, and it has many white settlements. Some have been there for three hundred years or more. In fact, the Portuguese have been plying these coasts since the 1400s. But that's only the outer edge of Africa, the crust. What's in the middle of Africa? What are the people like? Who are they? What do they think? We really don't know. Even when the slave trade was at its height, it was the coastal tribes that went inland and captured the inland tribes and brought them back to the coast to be traded. White men never went into the interior to get the slaves themselves. A few brave men like David Livingstone have gone inland, but not many of them have lived to tell about it. Those who have have seen only a little of what there is to see." With that Mr. Thomson buttered his bread and topped it with marmalade.

"But surely the Calabar mission knows something about the inland tribes?" Mary probed.

"Well, in 1846 when the Reverend Hope Waddell started the mission at Calabar, white people had never been more than five miles inland."

Mary was stunned. "Do you mean to say that the natives had been trading with white people for four hundred years and no one had ever gone more than five miles inland?"

"That's exactly right. Until the missionaries arrived, the sailors didn't even venture off their ships. Native canoes paddled up alongside the ships and traded their wares out on the water."

"That's amazing!" replied Mary. "Just what do we know? How far have the missionaries gone inland now?"

Mr. Thomson continued. "Let me see. I'd say about thirty-five miles inland. It's still very dangerous, you know. The natives won't even pass into each other's territory. Most tribes kill outsiders on sight."

Mary had a lot to think about, and she ate the rest of her meal in silence. The thing that troubled her most was that the people who obviously needed the gospel message the most were the ones who would kill anyone who brought it to them. She might be only a junior missionary, but right there, Mary Slessor set her sights on what seemed an impossible goal—going inland where no white person had been before.

The ship had been sailing for a week when Mary heard a sailor yell, "Land ho to port." Mary and the other passengers rushed to the left side of the ship to catch a glimpse of the first land they had seen since England. Mary squinted into the distance, and there, above the horizon, she could just make out the outline of land.

"Cape Verde," said Mr. Thomson, who was standing beside Mary. "That's Portuguese for Cape Green. It's the western most tip of Africa. Soon we will begin tacking to the east, skirting the coast of Sierra Leone, past the Ivory Coast, and on to Nigeria and Calabar."

"I can't wait," smiled Mary, excited to have finally laid eyes on Africa. She could hardly wait to set her feet on African soil. She had never seen an African person before. All she'd seen were drawings from Livingstone's books. Soon, though, she would be meeting Africans face to face and hearing their language in person.

"It will be easy to tell when we turn towards the coast," Mr. Thomson went on. "We'll be headed into a head wind, and the captain will order the engine to be fired up. The ship will need the extra power."

As the passengers stood silently in the hot tropical sun watching Cape Verde slip by, Mary rolled up the cuffs of her white blouse. She was hot in her long brown skirt and blouse. Beads of sweat were trickling down her back, and her sunbonnet was making her scalp feel prickly. She untied the ribbon under her chin that kept the sunbonnet in place.

"Now, keep that on," chided Mrs. Thomson. "A girl with your red hair and fair skin would burn to a crisp in an hour in this sun."

Mary retied the ribbon. It was true—she had the wrong complexion to be out in the sun without a bonnet.

After Cape Verde passed from view, the ship stayed too far out to sea to spot any more land. It was several hours later before the coast of Sierra Leone finally came into view. Mary was surprised to see that the hills were green, as green as the hills around Aberdeen, where she had spent her early childhood. She ran to get the Thomsons, and together they watched the coastline loom larger until Mary could make out rows of square, white cottages dotted on the hills, and below them, long white beaches fringed with swaying palm trees.

The lunch bell rang, but Mary would not leave the deck. She did not want to miss one minute of the coastline. She was enchanted by the scene, which looked to her like the setting for a fairy tale.

Several days later, on Saturday, September 11, as Mary peered down at the water, she noticed it had become a reddish brown color. The captain had told her to watch for silt, the first sign that they were approaching the mouth of the Cross River. Once again, Mary's heart beat fast with excitement. This was going to be the day she set foot in Africa, the day when she would finally see the people she was determined to live and die for.

By now all the passengers were on deck, craning their necks to be the first to spot Parrot Island in the entrance to the Cross River channel. At last someone sighted it just as the *Ethiopia* adjusted course to stay in the main channel.

Thick rows of strange, low trees with twisted gray trunks and roots that reached out like claws into the water lined the western shore of the river. Mary could not see the eastern shore because at its mouth, the Cross River was twelve miles wide.

"Mangroves," said Mr. Thomson, pointing to the strange trees. "Those trees are mangroves. They grow all the way up the river, and they're nearly impossible to penetrate."

Mrs. Thomson joined in. "Malaria comes from living too close to the mangrove swamps, doctors think. It has something to do with the dampness of the climate. That's why it's good the mission house is set up on a hill."

The passengers stood silently for a while, the vibrating steam engine thumping away beneath their feet. Flocks of colorful parrots swept over their heads, and crocodiles slipped effortlessly into the water, leaving only their beady eyes visible as the ship glided by. Mary knew the names of many of the animals from drawings in the books she had borrowed from the church library in Dundee, but no black-and-white etching could have prepared her for the amazing, colorful array of strange creatures she saw that morning. She studied the unfolding scene with utter fascination.

"See over there," Mr. Thomson interrupted her thoughts. "Those fences are what's left of the barracoons, the enclosures where slaves were kept penned while they waited for shipment. More slaves were shipped out of Calabar than any other port in the whole of Africa."

Mary winced. She imagined the slaves huddled together, men, women, and children, all chained like animals awaiting export. She was glad that the horrible practice had long since ended but sad that it had ever started in the first place.

Twenty miles up the Cross River, the *Ethiopia* swung to starboard and headed into a side river, the Calabar. The Calabar River was much narrower than the Cross, and Mary was able to stand on the aft deck and watch the wildlife on both sides of the river. About ten miles up the Calabar River, the ship steamed around a bend and Duke Town, tucked in a hollow beneath an enormous grove of cottonwood trees, came into sight. Small mud huts with palm thatched roofs stood beside sturdier, painted wooden houses. Along the edge of the river lay a ship's graveyard, a row of old ships that had been sailed out from England and tied up permanently at the water's edge. Traders used the old ships to store their palm oil and other cargo while awaiting a ship to carry it back to England. Some traders even used the old ships as homes now that many of them had taken to staying in Duke Town year-round instead of returning to England with each shipment.

Weaving in and out between the old hulks were canoes of every size and description. Some were laden with colorful cloth, others with tropical fruits and foods. On the hill above the town stood what Mary knew must be the mission house. It felt strange to Mary to finally see the house after having followed the mission's progress for the past twenty years. Before the mission arrived, the site had been used to dispose of the bodies of dead slaves. Now a conglomeration of mission buildings stood proudly at the top of the hill. For a moment, Mary wished she could draw—she would have liked to have had this first image of Duke Town down on paper.

The captain was standing at the railing to say farewell to Mary and the Thomsons as they were lowered over the side of the ship into a long boat called a gig. Six native boys with glistening muscles and gleaming white teeth paddled the boat to the mission beach. A second canoe followed with the luggage. Mary was amazed at how dark the young African men were, especially compared to her pale complexion.

Soon Mary felt the canoe bottom scrape along the sand and then come to a stop. She stood up, hitched her dress over her ankles, and climbed out. She stood still, taking in the moment. Mary Slessor was finally standing on African soil. Behind her, the *Ethiopia* had already weighed anchor and was maneuvering to turn around and head back out to sea and on south to its next port of call. Before her was her new home—or the white man's grave, as people back in Scotland had referred to it when trying to dissuade her from going. But now she was here, and Mary did not intend for it to be her grave.

Chapter 6

The Task Ahead of Her

Mary tried to push her hair into place under her sunbonnet as she followed the Thomsons up the flower-edged path to the mission house. She could feel the path swaying beneath her. After thirty-six days aboard ship, her body had become used to constant motion, and even though she was on land now, her brain was still telling her everything was swaying. The captain had told her that this was quite normal and in a few days she would regain her sense of balance and get her "land legs" back.

As Mary and the Thomsons approached the house, the large mahogany doors swung open and a group of chattering people poured out to greet the new arrivals. Mary felt suddenly shy, especially after the enthusiastic greeting. She hung back a little but was soon welcomed and drawn into the group. There were so many names and faces to remember, though she already knew many of the names from reading the *Missionary Record* back in Dundee. She especially recognized the name of the Reverend Alexander Ross, who was presently in charge of the mission, and Alexander Morton. An older woman introduced herself to Mary. "Welcome to Calabar, Mary. I'm Euphemia Sutherland. Let me show you your room, and then we'll all have a cup of tea on the verandah."

Mary smiled shyly and followed Mrs. Sutherland into the house.

The house interior was large and airy. The hardwood floors were highly polished, and there were large windows on every outside wall. Several pieces of solid mahogany furniture adorned the interior. The house had an air of efficiency about it, and Mary felt immediately at home. The two women climbed the stairs, and Mrs. Sutherland stopped outside a door in the hallway. "This is going to be your room," she said. "I'll leave you to get organized. Come on down whenever you are ready. I'll be out on the verandah."

"Thank you," smiled Mary. "I won't be long, I don't have much to organize," she said, pointing to the small carpetbag she was carrying. "Most of my things are in the trunk, which has still to be brought up to the house."

Mary stepped into her new room. The room was small, perhaps twice the size of the iron framed bed that stood at one end, but big enough for a lone missionary. The only other furniture in the room was a desk and a chair. All four of the bed legs were sitting in small cans of liquid, as were the desk legs. Mary bent down and sniffed the liquid. It was kerosene. Then she remembered. One of the missionaries home on furlough in Scotland had talked about keeping ants at bay, and kerosene, it turned out, was one of the few things ants didn't like. Cleverly, someone in the house had devised a way to isolate the furniture from ants with kerosene.

Mary put her carpetbag on the bed and walked to the window. She pushed the shutters open to reveal a panoramic view of a tropical paradise. She wished her mother and sisters could see it. Her room overlooked the mission garden. Large trees framed the garden's edges. Mary recognized orange and lemon trees, banana palms, and bright red hibiscus. But she had no idea what some of the other trees were. One was huge with shiny green leaves and perfectly round green fruit as large as pumpkins. Another had smaller oval fruit. Among the trees was a profusion of smaller flowering shrubs, the likes of which Mary had never seen growing in Scotland. One particular shrub produced colorful star-shaped flowers. Mary wondered if they were what was producing the wonderful sweet smell that wafted up to her room.

On the verandah below, Mary could hear the voice of Mrs. Thomson. Even though she would have liked to have stayed longer and taken in the beauty of her new surroundings, good manners required she go downstairs and join the others. The sun was beginning to set over the tropical jungle as Mary stepped out onto the verandah.

"Come and sit down, Miss Slessor," said Mr. Morton, standing to give her his seat.

One by one Mary was introduced to the missionaries who lived in the compound at Duke Town. There were four married couples, four single women, four single men, and Mrs. Sutherland, a widow. Mary learned that the Andersons, who normally oversaw the work of the mission, had just returned to Scotland for a brief furlough. Since Mrs. Anderson was not around, Mary was put under the care of Euphemia Sutherland.

Mary settled into her new life easily, and for the first week, being a missionary appeared to be a simple enough task. Mary had expected to get sick with some dreadful tropical disease right away, but from the day she stepped ashore, she felt fit and healthy. She had also expected the natives to be hostile and unwilling to listen to the missionaries, but instead she found the opposite. On her first Sunday in Calabar, she went to the morning service that was held in the mission chapel. The church overflowed with five or six hundred natives, and she was told another four hundred or so were gathered at churches in Old Town and Creek Town. The Reverend Ross conducted the service in the Efik language, and of course, Mary could not understand a word he said. She did recognize the tunes of several of the hymns they sung. The Africans seemed to enjoy the service greatly. Mary was impressed.

Mary was impressed with school on Monday morning, too. She was given a group of seven- to ten-year-old boys to teach. The boys all paid attention and tried hard to concentrate on the flash cards she held up. The boys were also polite and respectful, and Mary liked them from the start.

On Mary's second Sunday afternoon in Calabar, Mrs. Sutherland invited her to walk to Duke Town with her to visit some of the women's quarters, or "yards," as they were called. Mary eagerly accepted the invitation. She had seen the African children in school and the adults in church, and now she was eager to see them in their homes.

Together the two women strolled down the steep path to town. Their first stop was three men squatting beside the path. One of the men had his arm wrapped around five bottles of rum. His eyes narrowed when he saw two white women approach. Mrs. Sutherland, who had lived in Duke Town for twenty-seven years and spoke the Efik language well, began talking to the men. Mary listened carefully, trying to remember some of the strange nasal sounds that made up the Efik language. The discussion went on for several minutes until the three men got up and walked away.

Mrs. Sutherland turned to Mary and sighed. "It's the same old problem. So many of the men make their living selling rum to their fellow tribesmen, who then drink it and lie around for a day or so before they have to go and buy more. In the end, the money runs out, and they have to steal or loot from others to get more."

"What did you say to them?" Mary asked curiously.

"I told them God wants them to live good lives and look after their families, but they always reply with the same answer," Mrs. Sutherland said dejectedly.

"What?" asked Mary.

"They always say that white men bring them the rum and then white men tell them not to drink it. They say if rum is not a good thing, why would the same ships that bring the missionaries also bring the rum? It doesn't make any sense to them, and why should it? They think all white men are Christians, and then they see greedy traders selling them as much alcohol as possible. It's a difficult problem."

Mary could see that it was.

As the women continued down the path to Duke Town, mud huts came into view. Some of them were grouped together with fenced-off yards. At the first house the women stopped at they heard wailing. Mrs. Sutherland opened the gate in the fence and stepped into the bare yard. Mary followed. What she saw horrified her. Four people were lying around; they were filthy and thin. The yard stank, and Mary could see why. In the corner a group of huge flies buzzed in circles around a pile of human waste. The people were using the yard as a toilet!

Again Mrs. Sutherland spoke in Efik, her voice soft and gentle. When she had finished, she beckoned Mary to follow her inside the thatched hut. Mary ducked her head and entered. Inside, a ragged muslin curtain fluttered in the breeze. On the ground was spread a rectangle of cloth that was covering some kind of mound. Around the cloth was a variety of fruits and vegetables.

Mrs. Sutherland pointed to the cloth. "This family is in mourning," she explained. "They lost a little boy last week. This is his grave."

Mary shuddered. She couldn't imagine having a person's grave right beneath the living room floor.

"The Efik mourn by starving themselves and their families while they leave large amounts of food in the house for the dead person's spirit to eat," Mrs. Sutherland informed her.

Mary looked at the food. She supposed it would be rotten in a couple of days.

"The father is very angry," Mrs. Sutherland went on. "The Efik believe everyone is meant to die of old age, and if a person dies young, it is because someone else has put a curse on him. The father thinks he knows who 'killed' his son, and as soon as the mourning is over, he's going to kill the person. I was trying to tell him that sometimes young people die and it isn't anyone's fault. But he won't believe me. Their belief that evil spirits control everything that happens to humans is very strong."

Mary began to see that being a missionary here was not going to be so easy after all.

The two women reemerged into the bright sunlight. Mrs. Sutherland said a few words in Efik, and then she and Mary left the yard. Mary took some deep breaths of fresh air once she thought she was far enough away from the hut.

"Well," said Mrs. Sutherland, "why don't I show you something a little more cheerful? How would you like to meet a bride?"

"It sounds interesting," replied Mary, "as long as she's not surrounded by dead bones!"

The women walked past several more huts until they reached a hut surrounded by a high wall.

"This is the fattening hut," said Mrs. Sutherland. "The people of Calabar have an unusual tradition; they fatten up their brides before they get married."

Mrs. Sutherland yelled a few words through the stick fence, and a gate opened from the inside. She smiled and motioned for Mary to step through.

Inside, Mary saw two enormous African women. She imagined they must weigh at least two hundred fifty pounds each. The women sat on low stools that were partially engulfed in the folds of their flesh. Between the two women sat a huge platter of fried fruit. Several older women came out of the hut and greeted the missionaries. Once again, Mrs. Sutherland spoke in Efik. This time, though, she took out her Bible and read several verses to one of the fattening brides.

Mary could scarcely take her eyes off the two brides-to-be. She found it hard to believe they were deliberately making themselves fat. Mrs. Sutherland explained to her that in Calabar, a fat bride meant that her father had enough wealth to supply his daughter with endless amounts of food and that he had so many slaves she didn't have to do any work. The brides were to stay secluded in the fattening hut for up to a year, with only the old women to keep them company.

It made some sort of sense to Mary, though she could hardly believe that any man would find a woman that enormous attractive. Mrs. Sutherland assured her that the brides would not stay that fat. Once they were married, their husbands would not feed them so well.

By the time Mary left the fattening hut, her mind was spinning. Seeing the African people in church or school was one thing. It was quite another to see them in their own huts, following their own customs and way of life.

The two missionaries decided to make one more stop before heading back to the mission house. For Mary, this third visit was the most disturbing of all. The women were met at the gate by an old man who was chewing and spitting some sort of white fiber. Mrs. Sutherland spoke a few words to the man, who disappeared inside.

"It's ironic," Mrs. Sutherland said as she and Mary waited by the gate, "but slave women are free to move around Duke Town and talk to whomever they wish, but married women and widows have to ask their husband or their guardian if they can talk to anyone, and they are virtually never allowed out of their yards."

Mary sighed and looked around. The yard was a square about twenty feet by twenty feet. A small shrine was at the far end, with some yams on a low table and a dead chicken dangling upside down from a hook. It was the same thing Mary had seen in each of the other yards—an altar to placate the demons who tormented the house and the people living in it.

Finally the man, who Mary supposed was a guard, returned and motioned for the two missionaries to go inside the hut.

The hut was almost pitch black inside, and it took a moment for Mary's eyes to adjust. As they did, Mary began to make out the shape of a tiny, wizened old woman at the far end of the room. The woman smiled a toothless smile and beckoned the missionaries to come closer. Mary shuddered. The old woman reminded her of a witch in one of her childhood fairy stories. She was surrounded by human skulls and all sorts of tiny pouches and bones. Mary guessed it all had something to do with demons, but she wasn't sure what.

For once Mary was glad she did not speak Efik, because it meant she would not have to say anything to this strange old woman. Mrs. Sutherland talked to the woman for a while. The old woman spat on the floor as she listened.

Mary began to look around the room. In the far corner lay a large pile of rags, or so Mary thought, until the top layer began to move. Mary walked over to see what was there. Suddenly, a young woman sat up, and then two others. They were all very thin and looked half drugged. Mary smiled as best she could and said hello. The three young women made no attempt to answer her. Even when Mrs. Sutherland came over, they would not talk to her.

Ten minutes later, the visit was over, and Mary was glad to be out in the open again. Something about the hut had made it feel more oppressive than the others they'd visited.

"What was that all about?" Mary asked as she and Mrs. Sutherland began the walk back up the hill to the mission house.

"Those women are the widows of one of the richest men in town. The old one I was talking to was the senior widow, and since her husband died, she has been putting evil spells on the younger wives," Mrs. Sutherland replied.

"And starving them to death, it looks like," Mary added.

"I wouldn't be one bit surprised," agreed Mrs. Sutherland. "The senior wife has all the power over the younger ones. Often they stay in mourning for years, and many of them do die. There's not much we can do about it, I'm afraid. Only thirty years ago, they would all have been killed along with their husband and buried in his grave so they could keep him company in the afterlife."

The women walked on in silence for a while, Mary trying to take in everything she had seen that afternoon. The family in mourning, the brides in the fattening hut, the old widow holding the younger ones captive. "But don't most of these people go to church?" she finally asked, struggling to make sense of it all.

Mrs. Sutherland stopped and turned to face Mary. "Yes, it's true they do. We have over a thousand people coming to church, but in all the years the mission has been open, we've had only 174 natives actually say they wanted to become Christians."

"Why so few?" asked Mary.

"Well," continued Mrs. Sutherland thoughtfully, "most of the men have more than one wife—some have twenty or thirty—and they don't want to give them all up as the church would require them to do. And...," she paused to swat a mosquito that had landed on the back of her hand, "they want enough white man's religion to educate their children and make them look respectable, but deep down, most of them are still afraid of evil spirits."

Mary thought about Mrs. Sutherland's words. It had been thirty years since the mission in Calabar had opened, and in that time, about twenty missionaries, including Mrs. Sutherland's husband, had died there and been buried in the little cemetery. Another twenty missionaries had gone home to

Scotland with their health and, in many cases, their spirits broken. And all for fewer than two hundred converts! As she climbed the hill to the mission house, Mary was beginning to understand the enormity of the task ahead of her. Africa was every bit as foreign as she had imagined it would be. Mary wondered how she'd ever be able to get the gospel message across to these people.

Chapter 7

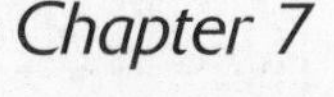

The Steady Plod

Splash. Splash. Mary shut her eyes and listened to the rhythmic movement of the paddles as they hit the water. It was almost too good to be true. She had been at the mission compound in Duke Town for three months now, and at last she was free. She was on her way upriver to visit Creek Town. Best of all, she was away from the confines of mission compound life, with its endless afternoon teas with government officials and formal dinners with the captains and officers of the trading ships anchored in the river. It was all too restrictive for Mary, who loved to be out with the local people learning their language, which she was picking up surprisingly fast. Mary didn't like dressing up in her maroon skirt and white blouse with the prickly collar and discussing the weather or the latest gossip from England. Such activity seemed pointless when there was missionary work to be done!

It had taken Mary several weeks to convince the Reverend Ross that she should be allowed to take a trip upriver. In the past, women missionaries had never been allowed to venture inland alone, but Mary was persistent, and in the end her persistence won out.

Now, away from Duke Town, everything around Mary felt fresh and wonderful. Even the crocodiles that glided menacingly around the canoe did not worry Mary. Of course, it helped to know that the boys paddling the canoe knew how to handle themselves around crocodiles. Mrs. Sutherland had also instructed Mary on how to avoid leopards and recognize deadly snakes!

The group arrived upriver in Creek Town in time for church on Sunday. Mary was eager to attend and meet the legendary King Eyo Honesty VII. The king had been one of the Reverend Hope Waddell's earliest converts, and Mary had read about him often in the *Missionary Record*.

King Eyo welcomed Mary and the boys and gave them seats of honor at the church service. The king looked very handsome in his silk waistcoat and gray pinstriped trousers, though he was not wearing a shirt or shoes. Mary envied him. Given the oppressive heat, she wished she could take off a few layers of clothing, but doing so would not have been proper for a Victorian woman.

The church service inspired Mary. The congregation listened enthusiastically, clapping and laughing in response to King Eyo's sermon. Native drums beat out powerful rhythms to the hymns that everyone sang with gusto. After the service, King Eyo approached Mary and asked her to join him for a meal at his palace. Mary could hardly believe it. She was going to eat with a king!

"I have no doubt you would like to see Creek Town," King Eyo said. "I will have one of my assistants guide you. When you hear the cannons, you will know that dinner is about to be served."

"Thank you so much," Mary replied, startled to hear such perfect English coming from an African man.

Mary followed the king's assistant through the alleys and streets of Creek Town, which was much like Duke Town, though not quite so crowded or smelly. As the pair walked along, most children ran and hid when they saw Mary. Mary was puzzled by their reaction until the king's assistant pointed to her red hair. "Fire," he said. "The white ma looks like her head is on fire."

Mary laughed. Even in Scotland her red hair had been a topic of conversation. No wonder the children of Creek Town were terrified by it.

Boom. Boom. The cannon fire caught Mary off guard.

"The king is summoning us," said her guide, pointing towards the rambling house overlooking the bay. "Follow me."

Soon Mary and her guide were ushered into a large room. Woven mats covered the floors and walls, and a huge dining table ran the length of the room. Seated at the head of the table was King Eyo, looking splendid in a black top hat he had apparently worn just for the occasion. He motioned for Mary to sit at his right side which she did nervously. She had no idea what the correct manners for a dinner like this were or what might happen if she did the wrong thing!

For the first half of the meal, Mary was extremely tense. Since she was the king's honored guest, she was the first to be served each course. As a result, she had no one to follow in what to do. She guessed correctly when a servant woman, wearing nothing but a flowery skirt, brought her a pitcher of water. Since there was no cup, Mary put out her hands to have them washed. The servant poured water over them, and a second woman came with a towel and dried them. Mary said a silent prayer of thanks—she had done the right thing with the water pitcher. She braced herself for the food that was sure to follow. Since she knew it would be an insult to the king to not eat the food offered her, she took a little from every platter. She recognized some of the food—roast goat, chicken, yams fried in oil, and green, leafy vegetables that resembled spinach. Sometimes, though, she had no idea what she was eating. One dish had tiny bones strewn among the meat. Was it a bird or a rat? Mary didn't know. Another dish was soup with a jellolike substance floating in it. Mary concentrated on her conversation with King Eyo as she gulped it down.

At one point in the conversation the king looked puzzled. "You appear to know a lot about me," he said to Mary in a questioning voice.

"Yes, I do, King Eyo," she beamed. "Everyone in my church in Dundee has read about you and the honest way you govern your people. Why, my mother has prayed for you every Sunday for as long as I can remember."

King Eyo stared at Mary, his eyes wide with surprise. "There are those in Dundee who know me?" he said incredulously. "And your mother cares for a king four thousand miles away?"

"Yes," replied Mary enthusiastically. "We all belong to God's kingdom, and many people are very interested in you."

The king was silent for a long moment. "I would like to write to your mother," he said. "Will you give me her address?"

Mary smiled. "Of course," she said, thinking how thrilled her mother would be to get a letter from King Eyo himself.

Mary spent several more days in and around Creek Town before heading back down the river to the mission compound at Duke Town.

In early January, William and Louisa Anderson returned from their stay in Scotland. They were veteran missionaries, and both were people of action. Mrs. Anderson, or Mammy, as she insisted everyone call her, was a whirlwind of activity. She seemed to have tried her hand at everything from building roads to negotiating peace treaties to nursing sick seamen. To Mammy, life was run by the clock. Even in Calabar, where the only time the local people knew was sunrise and sunset, Mammy Anderson tried to impose civilization through accurate timekeeping. This was not always successful outside the mission compound—the natives thought nothing of being an hour or two late for a meeting—but inside the mission, the clock ruled supreme.

As much as Mary admired Mammy Anderson's tremendous energy, she was not very good about being on time herself. As soon as Mammy arrived back in Calabar, she gave Mary the worst possible of all jobs: ringing the bell for morning prayers at 6 A.M. Mary had no way of waking up at that time each morning, and once, she had managed to stagger out half asleep and ring the bell at 3 A.M. She had mistaken the bright moonlight for sunrise! No one was happy with her that morning.

Another time, Mary was late to dinner, and according to Mammy's rules, anyone who was not present at the beginning of the meal did not get to eat until the next meal. Mary accepted her punishment and retired to her room for the night to await breakfast. An hour later, she heard a soft knock on the door. Mary opened the door, and there stood the Reverend Anderson with a tray of biscuits and tea. The reverend handed the tray to Mary and smiled. Mary whispered thank you, and the Reverend Anderson crept away as quietly as he had come.

It took Mary a while to get used to the iron hand of Mammy Anderson, but Mammy Anderson accomplished so much that Mary grew to respect her tremendously. After a year they were great friends, although Mary still did not dare to be late to dinner.

Life for Mary fell into a regular pattern. She taught school during the week, and after school or on the weekends she visited with women and children in their yards. She also went to visit King Eyo Honesty in Creek Town fairly regularly. The king was always delighted to welcome her into his palace.

Despite Mary's activity, something was missing. The townspeople Mary spoke to had heard the gospel message so many times they could repeat the Bible verses and tell their favorite Bible stories as well as she could. They made a big show of coming to church on Sunday, yet when Mary challenged them about their sacrifices to various gods and their treatment of each other, they were unwilling to change their ways. They still believed that evil spirits ran their lives. They didn't see anything wrong with human sacrifice or owning and killing slaves at will. Mary grew frustrated trying to get them to see their need for change. Over time, she began to understand that many of the natives were sly, telling the missionaries what they wanted to hear to win favor with the trading captains. Yet she kept sharing the gospel message with them, trying to be wise to their ways. But what she dreamed of was traveling into the interior and sharing the gospel message with people who had never had the opportunity to hear it.

Mary knew it would take a miracle for a single woman to be allowed to go alone into the unmapped areas of Calabar. She felt trapped, so close to the "real" mission field as she saw it, yet unable to go there. She prayed that a way would open up for her to go, but her prayers seemed to go unanswered. Instead, she became ill, very ill, with malaria. At that time, no one knew what caused malaria, so there was no way to avoid catching it. It was every missionary's dread. The only treatment was quinine, a medicine that was so strong it could kill a person as easily as cure her.

For days, Mary drifted in and out of consciousness. Sometimes she felt so cold her teeth chattered and her body shook uncontrollably. Other times she was so hot she thought her bed must be on fire. Mammy Anderson took special care of her, and eventually it became clear that Mary had escaped death at the hands of the disease.

Finally, one morning, Mammy Anderson came bustling into Mary's room and drew the curtains, letting in a stream of golden morning sunlight. "It's such a lovely day," she said brightly.

Mary squinted at the light. "Umm," was all she could manage to say.

"Well, it looks like you're getting better. We thought we'd lost you a time or two, lass," Mrs. Anderson said, leaning over to fluff Mary's pillows. Then matter-of-factly she said, "Your timing couldn't have been better. I went ahead and booked you passage on a steamer leaving for Liverpool next Friday. I almost thought I'd have to cancel it, but you'll be well enough to walk on board by then. You can use the voyage to recuperate. What with the cool air, you should be a new person by the time you get to Liverpool."

"But...," Mary tried to say weakly.

"No buts about it; you need a furlough," said Mammy Anderson cutting Mary off. "I know you've been here only three years, and it's a year earlier than you had scheduled to go home, but Scotland will do you good. In a year or so when you're feeling ready, you can come back to Calabar."

Mary lay still in bed. Every muscle in her body ached as she tried to take in the news. She was going home next week; that was a fact. She knew there was no arguing with Mammy Anderson once she'd made up her mind. But Mary wasn't going home the way she wanted to, as a healthy missionary with stunning stories to tell. Instead, she was going home a sick woman beginning to doubt she had done any good at all in Calabar. She had no great missionary tales to tell, only accounts of the steady plod of teaching boys the alphabet and visiting illiterate women in their yards. The last thing Mary wanted at that moment was to go home.

Chapter 8

Old Town

Mary sat quietly in the leather seat as the train jolted and swayed its way from Liverpool to Dundee. As the Scottish countryside rolled by, she tried to rest. A large crowd would be at the train station to welcome her. Mary knew that from experience, having been part of church groups who greeted returning missionaries in years past. As the train rolled along, she caught a glimpse of herself in the reflection of the window. Although she had rested on the voyage home, she still looked gaunt and old, and she could walk or stand for only a few minutes before having to sit down and catch her breath and gather her strength. She hoped her appearance would not shock people too much, especially her mother and sisters.

Finally, the long journey came to an end, and the train jerked to a halt at the Dundee railway station. The waving crowd was waiting for her. Mary pulled herself to her feet and made her way out to greet them. Her mother was standing at the front, and Mary collapsed into her arms, glad to be home.

Mrs. Slessor took her daughter straight home and made her a strong cup of tea. Mary's sisters, Susan and Janie, fussed over Mary, and after a few days, she felt well enough to venture out and walk to the end of the row of tenement houses and back. As she recuperated in the care of her mother and sisters, Mary came to a conclusion. Living in a tenement house with no running water, a shared toilet in a back garden, and a parade of dubious neighbors was no life for anyone. She wanted her mother and sisters to move out of Dundee into one of the villages that surrounded the city. Her mother and sisters thought it was a great idea. In fact, they had considered it themselves in the past, but they didn't make enough money among them for it to be possible.

As Mary lay on the couch week after week, she came up with a plan to help make it possible. All United Presbyterian missionaries in Calabar were given the same amount of money—sixty pounds a year—to live on. Living at the mission station in Duke Town, though, was expensive. Everyone there helped pay for all the entertaining of Europeans guests as well as for the many servants who cooked and cleaned the house and the expensive imported food they all ate. This meant that Mary spent nearly every penny of her yearly income.

Mary began to add up the money she could save and send home if she didn't live in Duke Town. As she thought about it, she realized she would never be happy in such a "civilized" place. She longed to be out in the jungle sleeping in a mud hut and cooking over an open fire. She wondered whether there was a chance she might be allowed to do so. She had, after all, survived her first term in Calabar, something many other missionaries had not managed. She decided to ask for another assignment, this time in a more remote place. If she lived and ate like the natives, she would need hardly any money at all. Then she would be able to send most of the sixty pounds a year home to help pay the rent on a cottage for her mother and sisters.

After six months at home, Mary felt strong enough to take walks out of the city into the green, misty countryside. It was so peaceful there. On these walks, Mary thought about how she would handle speaking in churches around Scotland. Speaking in front of a large audience of adults had always been difficult for Mary. Sometimes her stomach got so tied up in knots she was unable to talk at all and someone else had to speak for her. This had not been so much of a problem when she had itinerated with the other two Marys before leaving for Calabar. They had both enjoyed speaking, and since they all traveled together, Mary left it to them to do the public speaking. Now things were different. Now that she was feeling better, the mission board would arrange for her to speak in a hundred or more churches around Scotland.

Early in 1880, Mary began her speaking tour. She would sooner have faced a leopard alone in the jungle than the crowds of people wanting to hear all about her missionary work in Africa. Somehow, she found the strength to speak. She decided it was best if she told stories to her audience, so she told them about King Eyo, about the witchcraft that ruled the lives of people in Calabar, and about the little boys in school who were learning to read the Bible.

When people asked Mary what she wanted to do when she returned to Africa, she told them the truth. More than anything, she wanted to go inland where no white person had settled before and work among natives who had never heard of Jesus Christ. The Okoyong people attracted her the most. In her heart, though, she knew there was little chance of her leaving the well-manicured lawns and tea parties of the mission compound in Duke Town. The Reverend Anderson did not approve of young, single women venturing off into the bush on their own, and his wife, with all her accomplishments and bravery, agreed with him.

Although Mary never overcame her nervousness at speaking to adult groups, she found herself quite at home talking to children, and she was much more successful at this. On a visit to the town of Falkirk, Mary visited the local school. Two girls, Janet Wright and Martha Peacock, were particularly inspired by what she had to say, and they asked Mary if she would write to them. Mary agreed, never imagining that she had actually inspired them to follow her to Calabar.

Finally, sixteen months after arriving home, the missions board decided it was time for Mary to return to Calabar. Mary wrote to the board begging them to allow her to move inland or, at the very least, out of Duke Town and into one of the empty mission stations that dotted the area. She waited nervously for a reply, but none came.

Meanwhile, Mary moved her mother and sisters out of the smoggy city into a sunny little country cottage in Downfield, a tiny village on the outskirts of Dundee. Mary promised that somehow she would send money to help support them, and of course, Susan and Janie still had their jobs at the cotton mill.

Mary sailed back to Calabar with the Reverend and Mrs. Goldie, who had also been home on furlough. The Reverend Goldie had lived in Calabar for many years and had compiled an Efik dictionary and translation books. Mary was glad for the opportunity to get to know him and to pour out her heart. The Reverend Goldie listened, and although he made no promises, he said he would do what he could to help her. He must have done something, because soon after Mary got back to Duke Town, she was told she'd been assigned to work in Old Town. She would be working alone and expected to make decisions for herself.

Mary was ecstatic. Old Town was only three miles from Duke Town, but it gave her the opportunity to try out her missionary ideas, and it was a step closer to the inland people. She wasted no time in packing her few belongings and asking a team of men to ferry her upriver.

As the men paddled, Mary thought about all she knew of Old Town. The town was not a place with a peaceful history, that was for sure. It was one of the four original towns where the Reverend Hope Waddell had begun his missionary work in Calabar back in 1846, but all had not gone well there. The chief, Willy Tom Robins, as he called himself, was a brutal man who would not listen to the missionaries. Instead, he chose to follow the customs of his ancestors. In 1855, Chief Willy had become ill and, realizing he was about to die, had all of his wives, daughters, slaves, and servants chained up inside his huge compound. He gave instructions to his oldest son that they were all to be killed when he died. And they were—hundreds of them. British traders in the town were outraged and convinced the British consul to bring a gunboat up the river and shell the town. The consul gave the missionaries enough warning so they could evacuate the town before it was bombarded. What the gunboats did not destroy of the town, the fire that followed did. Since then, the inhabitants of Old Town had rebuilt most of the town, but they still held a grudge against the British. While missionaries had been tolerated for short periods of time, they were hardly welcomed with open arms.

As Mary stepped from the canoe at Old Town, she glanced up to see a human skull dangling on a pole on the hill above her. She was startled. Was it a warning meant for her? She couldn't be sure, but a shudder went down her spine as she led the way to the tiny mud and palm thatch hut where the last missionaries had lived. The structure was dilapidated, empty, and dirty. Mary and the men who had brought her upriver set to work making it a home again. About an hour later, they were done. The dead leaves had been sluiced off the floor with buckets of river water, a small iron cot had been set up against the back wall, and the door had been reattached to its hinges. Mary was delighted. "Thank you so much," she said to the men. "You can go back to Duke Town now and tell them I'm all settled in."

There was not much more Mary needed to do before she could start her missionary work. She had already decided to live as much like a native as she could, and that cut out a lot of extra work she would have had to do to keep up European ways. She ate food she bought cheaply at the local market, such as maize, beans, yams, fruit, scrawny chickens, fish from the river, and, of course, palm oil. And because she was eating local food, the food was easy to store, unlike the butter, bacon, mutton, eggs, flour, and sugar that she had eaten in Duke Town and that had to be stored carefully to keep out moisture and bugs. Mary no longer needed to store such food but was able to go to the local market each day and buy fresh food. She could also employ a local girl to cook the food for her without her having to train her to make shepherd's pie or scones. The only thing Mary did not want to do without was her cup of tea in the morning, and she allowed herself this one luxury. The money she saved living this way she sent home to help support her mother and sisters.

Gradually the people of Old Town warmed to Mary. Mary already knew some of the local boys who had attended school in Duke Town at various times, and she made friends with their families. Mary's first concern was to get those boys back into school. She set up a classroom in Old Town as well as in the nearby villages of Qua and Akim. She also had a supply of medicines with her that she used to treat sick people. Before long, she was also being asked to mediate arguments between the local people.

One morning, not long after arriving in Old Town, Mary opened the door to her hut, and there, lying on the ground, was a tiny sleeping baby. As Mary picked up the child and cradled it in her arms, she looked around for some clue as to who had left it there and why. She found none. Holding the baby in one arm, she lit the fire she'd set the night before and made a pot of tea. She spooned some into the baby's mouth, wondering what to do next.

As the sun rose in the sky, Mary's helper arrived. "You have a baby," she said to Mary, not sounding one bit surprised.

"Yes, I do," replied Mary, "but I don't know where it came from."

The girl shrugged her shoulders as she squatted beside the fire. "You are a god-woman," she said. "The babies will be brought to you."

The statement did not invite further discussion. From living in Duke Town, Mary knew that at times there were many uncared-for infants in the villages. Human life was not valued very highly in Calabar, and no one could be bothered raising another woman's baby. If, for instance, a slave mother died, her young children were killed and buried with her. The people believed that slave babies weren't worth the effort to raise. Worse still were the twin killings. All over Calabar, the birth of twins was seen as an evil curse. Custom demanded that both twins be killed within hours of birth, and the mother was either killed or put out of her house. Since anyone who tried to help the mother was also cursed, most of those mothers who were not killed normally died within a week or two anyway.

Mary guessed that this baby's mother had died and some family member had brought it to her to raise. That night she thanked God for allowing the baby boy's life to be spared. Despite being separated from his mother and milk supply, the baby began to grow. Soon Mary was taking him with her on her Sunday rounds.

On Sundays, Mary employed two boys to carry a pole with a bell slung from it. When she got to a village, she would ring the bell and wait for people to gather. If they did not, she would go and find them and bring them back to the meeting area. She would lay out a tablecloth on a flat surface, open her Bible, and preach. After the service, people would beg Mary to visit the sick. It was normally nightfall before Mary and her entourage arrived back in Old Town, where one more service was held, this time in the chief's compound. Most of the village came to watch the little red-haired missionary speak to them in their own language.

Just as Mary's helper had indicated, many other babies followed the first, until Mary's single-room hut was filled to overflowing with babies in woven baskets. Mary made a special trip to Duke Town to ask for help. Her plan was for another single woman to come and help with the children and free her to continue preaching and treating illness. Mary would help the other missionary set up an orphanage and train some of the local girls as aides.

When Mary arrived at Duke Town, she knew there would be no helper for her in the near future. Sickness was once again claiming the lives of missionaries. Mary arrived just as Mammy Anderson fell ill. The Reverend Anderson had become sick first, and Mammy had nursed him tirelessly, just as she'd nursed Mary when Mary had malaria. The Reverend Anderson survived, but the strain of nursing him hastened his wife's death. Losing Mammy shocked everyone, including Mary. Everyone had assumed that Mammy could survive anything. Soon afterwards, Mrs. Sutherland, the woman who had taken Mary under her wing when she first arrived in Calabar, became ill and died. Mary sobbed loudly at her funeral. For the first time, Mary saw firsthand why Calabar was called the white man's grave. She wondered who would be next.

Chapter 9

Honored Guest

In late 1882, two men from the Foreign Missions Board in Scotland came to assess both the missionary work and the missionaries at Calabar. They spent several days with Mary, including a Sunday on which they followed her through the jungle from dawn to dusk as she made her regular rounds of the surrounding villages. By the end of their stay, the men were exhausted! One of them wrote of Mary in his report, "Her labors are manifold [many], but she sustains them cheerfully. She enjoys the unreserved friendship and confidence of the people and has much influence over them."

After the men from the missions board left, Mary began to get restless. In Old Town, she was living just on the edge of a vast, unexplored wilderness filled with people she wanted to teach and help. She hired some local girls to look after her babies and started making longer and longer treks along the jungle tracks that led inland. Sometimes she went alone. On these treks, she was mindful of the instructions Mrs. Sutherland had given her when she first arrived in Calabar. So while she walked, she made lots of noise so as not to surprise the wild animals, especially leopards, which normally attack only when caught off guard. Mary sang hymns as loudly as she could and clapped her hands and stomped her feet.

Mary's reputation went before her. More often than not, Mary found that people in the villages she visited had already heard of the "white ma" with the flaming hair, although her hair was no longer fashionably long, as it had been when she first arrived in Calabar. Since she found it hard to keep long hair washed and pinned up in such an environment, she cut it very short. The other missionary women were aghast, but Mary couldn't have cared less. It was more practical to have short hair, and that was all that mattered.

Early in 1883, Mary received an invitation from Chief Okon to visit him and tell his people about the white man's God. Chief Okon lived at Ibaka about twenty miles west of Old Town, along a swampy delta tributary of the Cross River. Mary eagerly accepted the invitation and began making plans. She sent word to Duke Town that she would need a canoe and paddlers to take her to Ibaka and collect her two weeks later. She planned to take the four oldest children in her care with her. She made arrangements for the younger ones to be taken care of while she was away.

Mary's friend King Eyo heard of her plan and sent his men to try to dissuade her from going. He pointed out that the invitation could be a trick and she could easily be taken captive. Or she could be eaten by crocodiles on the way, or her canoe could be attacked by a hippopotamus. But Mary was convinced she should go. In the end, King Eyo insisted on providing his own royal canoe and paddlers to transport her to the village. He told Mary, "I do not want you to arrive there as a nameless stranger to a strange people, but as a lady and as our mother."

Mary was humbled by the king's generosity and even more amazed when his canoe finally paddled into Old Town. King Eyo had about four hundred canoes, but he had sent his biggest and most lavishly decorated one to transport Mary. The canoe was forty feet long and about five feet wide. In the middle was a small shelter, where Mary and the children would be able to rest in the shade and sleep a little along the way. The king had even had the canoe freshly painted bright yellow and red, which probably accounted for why it arrived in the early evening instead of after breakfast as promised. Mary organized her few pieces of luggage in the canoe, and then she had eight sacks of rice—a gift for Chief

Okon—loaded aboard. Lastly, she lifted in the four children and then climbed in herself. Despite the late hour, they set off for Ibaka.

The people of Old Town yelled from the water's edge. "Be careful. Don't trust them. If they kill you, we promise to avenge your murder."

It was hardly a cheerful farewell, and Mary was glad when Old Town was out of sight. She knew the people were warning her out of concern, but they were beginning to make her nervous!

The jungle had an eerie quality to it at night. It was filled with unidentifiable sounds, which Mary tried not to think about. Instead, Mary chose to concentrate on the rhythmic chants of the paddlers, who sang on through the night. Three drums kept time, and a man in the back made up words to sing, "Ho! Ho! We are honored. Ho! Ho! We have our white ma with us. Ho! Ho! On we go into the night."

The children quickly fell asleep, and Mary, who was perched on a sack of rice, quickly found sleep as well.

The brilliant African sunrise the following morning came quickly, heralded by the trumpet of a distant elephant and the squawk of colorful parrots overhead. Mary rubbed her sleepy eyes, grateful to the men for paddling all night to get her to Ibaka. As the canoe rounded a bend in the river, there was the village perched on the side of a hill. A minute later, the canoe was scraping along the bottom of the silty river. Mary readied herself to clamber out of the canoe.

"No! No, White Ma! You must stay where you are," yelled the lead paddler, splashing through the water to get to Mary. "You are not to get wet. King Eyo said so. We are to carry you," the paddler explained as he beckoned to another man.

The two men fashioned a chair with their hands for Mary to sit on, and then they hoisted her out of the canoe and onto dry land. But they didn't put her down. To Mary's surprise, they carried her through the village, right to the chief's door. As they set her down, one of them said, "The people must see what an honor it is to have White Ma for a guest."

Mary was touched, but she noted that most of the villagers the paddlers had been trying to impress had run away and hid when they saw her. Once again she found herself in a place where most people had never seen anyone with blue eyes, red hair, and pink, freckly skin. Still, she was sure their curiosity would overcome their fear in the end and they would creep back to see what she was doing.

Chief Okon's servant ushered Mary inside, along with the four children, who trailed behind her. As she made her way inside, Mary overheard the paddlers impressing upon the chief's guards that they had better take care of her or there would be trouble when they came back to get her in two weeks.

The chief was grateful that Mary had come, and he spared nothing to make her stay as comfortable as possible, at least to his way of thinking. Mary spent most of the day eating and talking about the

Bible with Chief Okon and attending to the medical needs of his household. She lanced several boils, disinfected and dressed a number of open sores, and even stitched up a cut so that it could heal properly.

As she dressed wounds, Mary noticed she'd been right. People began to creep up and watch her. First it was just a few, but the number continued to grow, until it seemed that the entire village was following her from hut to hut. As Mary worked away, one of the chief's wives yelled reports on everything Mary did for those who were too far back to see her for themselves. If nothing else, Mary decided, she'd brought free entertainment to the village.

When night began to fall, Chief Okon showed Mary to his own room, where she and the children were to spend the night. The room had no door or windows, just holes where they would have been. Soon black heads were popping in and out of the holes, watching as Mary prepared herself and the children for bed. Mary did hang a blanket in the doorway while she undressed and got into her nightgown, but she took it down again afterwards, not wanting to appear to have anything to hide.

Mary had just finished singing the children to sleep when two of Chief Okon's fat senior wives waddled into the hut, laughing and slapping each other. Mary knew instantly why they were there. They were going to keep her warm by sleeping beside her! It was a custom in Calabar for honored guests to sleep between the fattened, well-oiled wives of the chief. A wave of revulsion swept over Mary, but she knew they meant her no harm. She forced herself to smile and welcomed them into the room. She lay down, and the two wives lay down, one on either side of her. Mary almost gagged at the heavy scent of coconut oil that hung over them all, but she felt it was important to respect their customs as long as they didn't conflict with anything in the Bible.

The chief's wives fell asleep almost immediately, snoring loudly while Mary lay sandwiched between them. As she lay there, Mary wondered what the church back in Dundee would say if they could see her now, or even how the missionaries in Duke Town would react. Mary knew her perspective was changing. She had begun to cross over from looking at what would be acceptable in Scotland to what was acceptable in Calabar. If God allowed her to live longer, Mary knew she would soon feel more at home among Africans than among Scottish people.

By midnight, Mary felt like she was suffocating. With no door or windows, there was no air movement in the room. Mary could hear rats scurrying over the thatched roof and unknown animals sniffing and snorting around the yard. Finally, just before dawn, she fell asleep.

Despite the lack of sleep, the days went by quickly. Mary continued to dress wounds and attend to sick people as well as hold Bible services each morning and evening. The local people were in awe of how well she spoke their language. Indeed, some people came just to hear a white woman with an "Efik mouth."

On the sixth night, a storm swept through the village without warning. The chief's hut was lit up by sizzling forks of lightning, and the wind roared through the door. The four children climbed into Mary's bed and squeezed themselves between Mary and the chief's wives. Things crashed and banged around them, but Mary knew it was safer to stay inside than to venture out. Suddenly there was a huge gust of wind, and the roof of the hut lifted into the air and disappeared. Mary, the children, and the chief's wives found themselves deluged with rain. The two wives began to cling to Mary just like the children. Mary knew that she had to take charge of the situation.

"Come on, children, let's sing," Mary yelled bravely over the wind and then began singing one of her favorite hymns. Soon everyone joined in. By the time the storm had passed, everyone was hoarse from singing. It was still dark, but one of the chief's servants brought a reed lamp for light. Next, the servants pulled a cloth over the rafters to form a makeshift roof. The box of clothing Mary had brought with her was still dry, and Mary found a change of clothes for each of the children. She settled them down on the platform bed with the chief's wives to keep them warm, then dried herself off and took a dose of quinine. She felt sure the drenching she'd just received would bring on another bout of malaria.

Mary was right. By morning, she had all the classic symptoms of the sickness—chattering teeth, aching bones, and inability to concentrate. The chief's wives, who had suffered no lasting effects from the storm, were very concerned for her. Mary gave them instructions on what to do with the children if she were to die, took another dose of quinine, and drifted back to sleep.

It was three days before Mary was well enough to get out of bed and leave the hut. When she did, she was shocked at the devastation the storm had caused. Just about every hut was damaged, and some were completely destroyed. Huge kapok trees had been uprooted and hurled onto their sides by the wind, and many canoes had been dashed to pieces or washed down the river.

Amid all of the commotion, Mary began to sense something else was wrong. She heard snippets of information whispered from one woman to another. Eventually, she got one of them to tell her what was going on. The storm had ripped a hole in the back fence of the wives' compound of one of the senior men in the village. Thirty of the man's wives were housed there, and the two newest wives, both sixteen years old, had escaped through the hole and spent the night with a young man from the village. The two had been discovered, and a special meeting, or *palaver,* as it was known, had been called to discuss punishment.

Of course, only the men of the village got to participate in the palaver, so the women waited tensely to see what the punishment would be. Mary waited with them. After an hour or so, the meeting came to a close, and Mary wasted no time in asking for an audience with Chief Okon.

"What did you decide to do with the girls?" she asked, getting straight to the point.

The chief, who would not have tolerated such a question from any of his own women, answered her directly. "They have done wrong. They will get one hundred lashes each."

Mary's mouth dropped open. She knew one hundred lashes meant nothing less than a long, slow death for the two girls. Their backs and legs would be shredded to pieces by the whip, and the infection that would set into the wounds would surely kill them. Mary had to think of a way to save them.

"Recall the palaver," Mary abruptly demanded in her most firm voice. "I want to speak on the girls' behalf." She held her breath, waiting to see what the chief's reaction would be.

"I cannot do that. The sentence has been set," Chief Okon replied.

"Did you ask me to come here and tell you about God?" Mary asked.

"Yes," replied the chief.

"Well then," she continued, "I wish to tell you what God thinks of the girls' behavior and of your punishment."

For a brief moment, Chief Okon looked confused, and Mary knew she had said the right thing.

"Very well," the chief finally sighed. "But the men will not be pleased to hear from you."

Fifteen minutes later, Mary was sitting cross-legged in the palaver hut. The two girls sat opposite. For a brief moment, Mary thought about the dangerous situation she had put herself in, but her concern for the girls gave her courage. She cleared her throat and spoke loudly. "I want to tell you girls that you have brought shame on your husband's house. You should not have run off in the night like you did."

The two girls looked shocked at what Mary had said, while the men all sat a little straighter, smiling and nodding as if to say, *So the white man's God agrees with us!*

The men did not smile for long. Next Mary turned to them. "It is disgraceful that you continue to take young girls to be your brides when you have all the wives and children you could ever need. The young women should be given to the young men in the village, not cooped up for the rest of their lives in a yard waiting for some old man to summon them."

Mary blushed as she spoke. Coming from Victorian Britain, she knew she was talking about indelicate matters that a well-bred woman would never talk about in front of a man. But she reminded herself that this was Africa and Africa was different.

The men began to yell at Mary, and Mary yelled right back at them! After an hour, tempers calmed, and the men agreed to reduce the girls' punishment to ten lashes each—that was as low as they would go.

Mary thanked the men and returned to her hut. At least the girls had a chance to live now if they received immediate care. As she opened her medical bag and took out several bandages and an amber bottle of laudanum, a powerful painkiller, Mary could hear the crowd gather, and then she heard the slash of a rawhide whip. She stood rooted to the spot, counting. One, two, three. Would Chief Okon honor his word? The first girl's piercing screams split the air. Eight, nine, ten. The lashes stopped, and Mary breathed a prayer of thanks and hurried out the door.

Several women were already half carrying, half dragging the first girl to Mary. Mary beckoned them inside, where they lay the naked girl on her bed, and went to retrieve the second girl, who was screaming loudly in the background with each lash of the whip. Mary went straight to work. She spooned some laudanum into the girl's mouth, then began tending the wounds.

The second girl arrived screaming and writhing in pain and was laid facedown beside the first girl. Within minutes, the floor was awash in blood as Mary cleaned the long, deep lashmarks that the whip had cut into the girls' backs and legs. Then Mary bandaged the wounds as best she could.

The two girls lay in Mary's room, where Mary tended to them for the remainder of her visit to Ibaka. When it was time for her to go, she showed one of the chief's wives how to change the bandages and look after the girls. Mary hoped the girls recovered fully, though she wasn't at all sure the men wouldn't hold another palaver and reverse their decision on the punishment after she had left.

After two weeks in Ibaka, which seemed more like a month to Mary, it was time for Mary to return to Old Town. The babies needed her, and it was time to start school up again. Chief Okon insisted that Mary travel home in his canoe, and he invited her to return as soon as possible. Mary assured him she would indeed return—and soon—but once again, sickness would change her plans.

Chapter 10

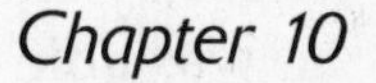

Janie

The local women wailed loudly and reached out to touch Mary as she was carried down to the canoe. It was March 1883, and Mary had become sick, too sick to medicate herself and wait for the illness to pass. To recover this time she needed to be in Duke Town, where she could get proper medical care.

Within the past month, two missionaries had died in Calabar. One of them was Samuel Edgerley, one of Mary's good friends. Samuel had gone to explore farther up the Calabar River. He had managed to get to Atam, 160 miles inland. On the way back, he had become ill and had to stop and rest in a village. Alas, the hammock he was sleeping in snapped in the night, dumping him onto the floor, where he hurt his back. Samuel's crew, not knowing what else to do, loaded him into the canoe and paddled all the way back to Duke Town. Samuel Edgerley died soon after arriving back and before he was able to tell anyone about what he had seen so far upriver.

Soon after this, Dr. McKenzie fell ill and died. He had been sick on and off for about a year, often needing to be carried to a patient's bedside so that he could diagnose the patient's condition and prescribe medicine.

Mary felt herself being laid gently into the bottom of the canoe ready for the trip downriver to Duke Town. She had already made arrangements as to what should happen to the children if she did not return—that is, all except for one child. Two weeks before, Mary had raced through the jungle in the middle of the night hoping to reach a pair of twins before they were killed. A woman from a neighboring village had risked her life to inform Mary of their birth. Mary arrived just as a hole was being cut in the back of the hut to pass the twins out. Since the villagers believed it meant extra bad luck to carry a twin baby out through the door of a hut, a special exit hole had been cut and then was mudded over later. The twins were still alive, and Mary raced into the hut, yelling wildly. She grabbed the two babies and ran back into the jungle, leaving behind a startled group of relatives who had come to witness the killing of the twins.

The relatives did not follow Mary back along the trail to Old Town. It was too dangerous to travel through the jungle in the dark of night. Mary, though, didn't care; she had the two babies tucked safely under her arms, and she prayed aloud and recited psalms as she ran. When she got back to her hut in Old Town, she lit a reed lamp and examined the twins—a boy and a girl—both small but healthy as far as she could tell. She ground up some plantains and mixed them with boiled water to feed the babies. Then she wrapped the babies up together and put them beside her in bed.

The twins flourished, and Mary's assistant helped her care for them. However, Mary had made a mistake. She had left the babies behind one Sunday while she made her preaching rounds of the surrounding villages. While she was gone, the family of the twins had tricked Mary's helper into "lending" them the baby boy. An hour later, the baby was found strangled to death on the jungle path. Mary wept when she heard the news and vowed not to let the little girl out of her sight. Now, as sick as she was, she insisted that Janie, as she called the little girl, go with her to Duke Town.

When Mary arrived at the mission compound in Duke Town, Dr. Hewan was there to meet her. He was a new doctor who had recently arrived in Calabar to study under Dr. McKenzie. Instead, he had found himself taking the doctor's place. Dr. Hewan treated Mary as best he could, but he held out little hope for her survival. When the monthly steamer arrived from England, he suggested she go back to Scotland on it. She would probably die on the voyage, he told her, but he was sure she would die anyway if she didn't leave Calabar. Mary agreed to go, on one condition—that she be allowed to take baby Janie with her.

Everyone at the mission compound, including the Reverend Anderson, thought it was the most ridiculous thing they had ever heard. What would happen to the baby if Mary died on the way back? Who would look after her? Mary listened to all their objections, but she would not budge. If she was to return to Scotland, it would be with the baby. Otherwise she feared Janie would be hunted down and killed by her family.

Eventually, the Reverend Anderson gave in to Mary's stubbornness, and Mary and the baby set out for Scotland. As the steamer chugged its way northward, Mary did not die; instead, her strength began to return. Mary didn't know why she was getting better, other than perhaps because she knew Janie needed her to live.

From the moment Mary stepped off the ship, Janie was the center of attention. Most people in the British Isles had never seen a black baby, and Janie was especially cute, with her curly black hair and ready smile. Mary couldn't walk down the street in Dundee without people stopping to stare at Janie and ask questions about her. This amused Mary, who thought about how the reverse happened whenever she visited remote African villages, where *she* was the oddity everyone came to see.

Mary's family loved Janie. Mrs. Slessor was particularly thrilled with her new "granddaughter" and looked after her and Mary. Janie was baptized at Wishart Memorial Church.

Finally, Mary's strength fully returned, and she was able to begin the dreaded round of speaking engagements in churches. This time, though, she had baby Janie with her, and that made all the difference. To the members of the audience, Janie was a piece of Africa they could touch and hold. She was tangible evidence that the missionaries did save lives and challenge barbaric customs. Everywhere Mary went, money poured in for the mission. Although this seemed like a good thing, in fact, it held Mary up from returning to Calabar.

By January 1884, eight months after she had arrived in Dundee, Mary felt well enough to return to Calabar. The Foreign Missions Board, however, insisted she stay longer and do more itinerating. It pointed out that the mission in Calabar needed more money and more recruits and that Mary's talks were providing an abundance of both. Reluctantly, Mary agreed to stay and visit more churches with Janie.

Although she hadn't really wanted to stay longer in Scotland, Mary was soon glad she did stay. Her sister Janie became very ill with tuberculosis, and Mary was able to help her mother nurse her. The doctor told Janie she needed to move to a warmer climate if she was to have any hope of recovery. Mary was desperate. Since she could not leave her sister when she was so ill, she came up with a plan. She asked the missions board for permission to take her sister with her to live in Calabar. The board refused. The plan would not have worked anyway, because Mrs. Slessor caught tuberculosis from Janie. The only healthy family member left was Mary's sister Susan.

Mary knew she could not return to Africa and leave her family in the condition they were in. She came up with another plan. She rented a house in Devon in the south of England, where the climate was warmer. Mary moved her sick mother and sister there while Susan stayed in Dundee for a few weeks to tie up the loose ends. Then the unbelievable happened! Mary received word that Susan had died. Susan had been staying in Dundee with a friend, who had found her dead in bed one morning. Mary, Janie, and Mrs. Slessor were devastated. Who would look after the two invalids now?

Mary hurried back to Dundee to bury her sister. While there she made a painful decision: She would stay in England with her family. Her missionary work in Calabar would have to wait until her mother and sister either died or recovered. It was a grim choice to have to make, but Mary could see no other option. She thanked God she still had baby Janie with her as a reminder of Africa.

When Mary returned to Devon, she told her mother about her decision. Mrs. Slessor was not at all happy about it. She could see that Mary's heart was in Calabar, and she didn't want her daughter's work to stop just because she was sick. She argued back and forth with Mary about the decision until in September 1885, Mary asked a Christian friend in Dundee to come to Devon and take over caring for her mother and sister. She offered to pay the friend from her allowance, which would resume as soon as she set sail for Africa. The friend agreed, and Mary began making plans to return to Calabar with baby Janie. She was convinced it would be the last time she would see her mother and sister, and it was a sad parting. Yet Mary knew that her mother, a stubborn Scot, would have things no other way.

In the afternoons aboard ship when Janie was tucked safely into her bunk for a nap, Mary would sit on deck and watch the sea break over the bow of the ship. She would think about Calabar, which was as much home to her as Dundee or Devon, perhaps even more so. Mary had looked forward to speaking Efik again and seeing her friends in Old Town. But this time she would not be living in Old Town. The missions committee had informed her of this just before she set sail. This time she was to be stationed at Creek Town.

Two missionaries, Miss Johnstone and Miss Edgerley (Samuel Edgerley's sister), had been living in Creek Town. Now they were both too sick to continue on there, and Mary had been asked to take their place. She could have said no, but not without a lot of misunderstanding, and so she agreed to the move. Besides, Mary could see some good things about being in Creek Town. It was the village of her friend and protector King Eyo, and she had many other friends there as well. Hugh Goldie and his wife were stationed there. Mary had grown to highly respect them over the years and looked forward to their company. Most important, Janie would be farther away from her family, who undoubtedly would still want to kill her. But there were also some drawbacks to being in Creek Town. Mary would have to live a more European lifestyle, entertaining white guests, eating English food, and dressing like a Victorian lady.

At thirty-seven, Mary still harbored the dream of living far out in the African bush, away from European influences altogether and ministering to Africans who had never heard the gospel message or of its power to free them from their oppressive customs. But Mary's dream was one that the missions board didn't support. Despite their opposition, Mary prayed that God would use her time in Creek Town as preparation for fulfilling her dream sometime in the future. She could not have imagined how dramatically her prayers would be answered or where her dream would lead her in the years ahead.

Chapter 11

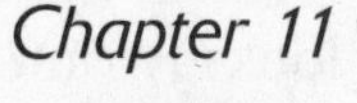

Creek Town

"Welcome home, Mary Slessor," bellowed the Reverend Anderson from the shore as the steamer maneuvered into its berth on the Calabar River. Mary waved to him while Janie peered cautiously from behind Mary's skirt. Janie didn't remember her homeland and was seeing it through the eyes of a three-year-old girl who knew only Scotland. It must have all seemed very strange to her, and Mary was anxious for Janie to reacquaint herself with her roots and learn to speak Efik.

Mary reached down and scooped Janie up into her arms. "It's all right, Janie," she said. "We're home, home in Calabar."

As she scanned the scene, Mary pointed to the new steam launch tied up at the new jetty in Mission

Hill Bay. "Look, Janie," she said excitedly, "there's the new boat the Sunday school children in Scotland saved up to buy. Isn't it grand? We'll have to write a letter to the children and tell them how wonderful it looks, won't we?"

Janie nodded.

It was December 4, 1885, and Mary was welcomed back into the missionary family with great enthusiasm. After all, she was one of the few missionaries who had survived two terms on the mission field in Calabar. Jessie Hogg, a young woman whom Mary had met in Scotland, was one of the first people to meet her. She had taken up the missionary challenge after hearing Mary speak, and it made Mary feel good to think her time in Scotland had not been wasted. In fact, as a result of Mary's efforts in Scotland, the mission now had more money than ever before and the new steam-powered launch to ply the rivers of Calabar.

Jessie Hogg wasn't the only new arrival at the Calabar mission. In the thirty-three months Mary had been away, five other new missionaries—three from Scotland and two from Jamaica—had arrived. This brought the total number of Presbyterian missionaries in Calabar to seven ordained ministers, their wives, four single men, and four single women.

After spending the weekend in Duke Town, Mary and Janie made their way to Creek Town for a lavish reunion with King Eyo and all Mary's Creek Town friends. The first question the king asked Mary was whether her mother was well. Mary had a letter for King Eyo from her mother which she handed to him. King Eyo and Mrs. Slessor had been corresponding regularly since Mary's first visit to Creek Town. Mary told the king she hoped her mother was fine, but in the pit of her stomach, she had a sickening feeling that things were terribly wrong.

In fact, they were. Mrs. Slessor died on New Year's Eve, just three weeks after Mary's arrival back in Calabar. Then three months after her mother's death, Mary received a letter notifying her that her sister Janie had also died. After she received the letter, Mary led a normally scheduled Bible study and then spent the rest of the night sobbing into her pillow. Within a year, she had lost her mother and her last two remaining sisters.

For many days Mary felt bitter and empty. She thought about all the decisions she had made. Had she made a mistake returning to Calabar? Should she have insisted on her sister's returning with her to Calabar? Why hadn't she realized how close to death her mother was and stayed home with her for two more months? Mary had many questions but no answers. Eventually, Mary accepted the fact that her family was gone. She wore her mother's wedding ring as a reminder of the people who had meant so much to her. The ring was a plain gold band worn thin by fifty years of hard work.

Once again, Mary Slessor threw herself into missionary work. And there was plenty to throw herself into. Miss Johnstone and Miss Edgerley had set up a busy schedule of visiting women in their yards, treating the sick, and teaching school and Sunday school. Since they had both become sick and had returned to Scotland, Mary took on both their workloads. Not only that, she continued to attract the usual collection of children. While she was in Scotland, new homes had been found for the children she'd left behind. Now that she was in Creek Town, other children were sent to her until she soon had five children as well as Janie living permanently with her, along with a number of others who drifted in and out of the house. The oldest girl was thirteen-year-old Inyang, who had been sent to Mary for training in running a European house in the hope she could one day get a job as a housemaid. Inyang was a big girl, much bigger than Mary, but gentle and amiable. Her one problem was that she didn't like to wear any clothes. Of course, this behavior startled some of the other missionaries who came to visit. Inyang soon took charge of the day-to-day running of the kitchen and helped take care of the other children.

Okin also lived with Mary. He was the eight-year-old son of a slave whose owner decided he should be brought up to know the Christian God. This decision puzzled Mary because the owner was not at all interested in Christianity. Still she was glad to take in anyone who was given to her.

Ten-year-old Ekim was the oldest boy living at Mary's house. One of King Eyo's sons, Ekim was a quick learner and was kind and patient. Mary considered it an honor to raise him. She hoped he would one day take on some influential role in the tribe.

Another boy was sent to live with Mary by King Eyo's sister. Someone had seen the boy's parents steal a dog from a neighbor and secretly cook and eat it and had told the dog's owner. The owner was furious. He had been hoping to eat the dog at a feast the following week. He went to the couple's house and laid a charm representing a curse at their front door. Within days, the woman fell ill and died, and the boy's father became too upset to care for his one-year-old son. Since the family was under an evil curse, no one else would feed or care for the boy either. King Eyo's sister had ordered that the toddler be taken to Mary. It took many weeks before the child was finally strong and healthy. When Mary sent word to the king's sister asking whether one of her slaves was willing to raise the child, the king's sister's compassion apparently ran out. The woman sent back a message saying, "Let the boy die." Mary did not. She kept him, and he too became part of her family. Along with these four children was a six-year-old girl who, with Janie, got into a lot of mischief.

One afternoon, not too long after Mary had settled into Creek Town, a runner reported to her that Janie's father was coming to visit her. Mary had heard that Janie's mother had died while they were away in Scotland, but she knew nothing of the father's whereabouts. Sure enough, a short time later, a tall man with huge hands and a frown on his face walked up to Mary and informed her that he was Janie's father. Mary's heart thumped in her chest. Mary wasn't sure what to do. Had the man come to take Janie away or, worse, to kill her on the spot? Perhaps he'd had bad luck lately and blamed Janie, a living twin, for it. As Mary said a quick, silent prayer, she felt she should let the man see his daughter.

"I just want to see her from a distance," the father explained.

"She won't hurt you," replied Mary, then turning to Inyang she said, "Go and bring Janie to me. Tell her she has a special visitor."

It was a tense few moments as they waited for Janie to appear. Janie ran straight to Mary and hid behind her skirt.

"Janie, this is your father," said Mary gently. "I want you to go over and give him a big hug."

Janie and her father shared a common look of terror, but Janie did as she was told. At first her father held her at arm's length, but then he hugged her tightly, tears running down his cheeks. Mary invited him to stay for lunch of rice and soup. When it was time to go, the father promised to return in two days. When he did, he brought with him food for the household. From that time on until he died a year later, he would walk great distances to bring his daughter and the white ma food.

King Eyo often called upon Mary's services. Mary understood British law better than he did, especially as the role of the British in Calabar was changing. Until this time, an agreement known as the Berlin Conference Agreement had given various European nations "spheres of influence" in Africa.

The Calabar region was under the British sphere of influence. This meant that the British were supposed to have control over the people and trading in the area. However, in 1887, Germany, which had long been interested in the Cameroons, claimed it by force, driving out the Baptist missionaries from England who worked there and shutting down their mission stations and schools. This move by Germany upset the whole fragile balance of spheres of influence, and other foreign governments began to flex their muscles over territory in Africa.

Of course, this situation greatly worried the missionaries and everyone else in Calabar. They wondered whether the Germans would march from neighboring Cameroon into Calabar. King Eyo was especially worried. He had an excellent relationship with the British, especially with Mary's help, and he had no desire to start all over again with another foreign power.

The British consul felt the best way to secure the Calabar region was to press inland with British troops and gunboats and open up more trade routes and impress the local inhabitants with the might of Britain. The missionaries, including Mary, pleaded with the British consul to let them to be the first to make contact with the inland tribes. They were convinced that many natives would be killed in unnecessary fighting if troops were sent inland first.

Mary Slessor was ready and willing to go inland. She had her heart set on going to Okoyong, situated in the triangle of land between the Cross and Calabar Rivers. When she told King Eyo this, he was horrified. Okoyong was the most savage region in all Calabar.

"Are you crazy?" he asked Mary. "You must listen to me. The Okoyong are not good people. They do not trust anyone, not even each other. They are always keeping watch in case they're attacked by their neighbors."

Mary nodded. "I know. They live in great darkness," she replied.

"They practice all the old ways—twin murder, trial by poison bean, and wife and slave killing. Just last week I heard one of their lower chiefs had died. They said he had forty people—slaves, children, and wives—buried with him," King Eyo pleaded. "Mary, they will think nothing of killing you if you tell them something they don't wish to hear."

Mary listened carefully to what the king told her. She knew the coastal and the Okoyong tribes had been at war for generations. The latest round of fighting had ended with the coastal group having the upper hand. The Okoyong offered to show that they were ready to surrender by burying a man alive. Since the Christian leaders at Creek Town would not agree to this, the two tribes had remained unofficially at war with each other. Still, nothing King Eyo said dissuaded Mary. Like her hero, David Livingstone, she wanted to go farther inland.

It looked as if Mary Slessor might never be allowed to pursue her dream of inland missionary work. But in 1881, the Foreign Missions Board in

Scotland had made a decision to allow single female missionaries to work more independently of men. This new plan was called the Zenana Scheme, and it immediately went into effect in India, China, and the West Indies. However, West Africa was considered a special case. Even the women on the Zenana committee thought it would be certain death for female missionaries sent out on their own in this region. However, five years later, with constant prodding from Mary, the committee reversed its decision on West Africa. In 1886, it decided to recommend that single women missionaries should be allowed to apply for inland posts where they would be working alone. Naturally, Mary was the first to apply.

The Zenana committee promised to review Mary's application, and in early 1888, Mary received a letter informing her she had permission to venture into Okoyong territory. Of course, only time would tell whether this permission would turn out to be a dream come true or an endless nightmare for Mary.

Chapter 12

To Ekenge

Leaving Creek Town was the saddest farewell Mary had ever experienced. The general mood felt like a funeral—her funeral! It had taken six months, but now in early August 1888, Mary was finally taking the enormous step of moving into Okoyong territory. After Mary had made three exploratory trips to the area, a chief there had begrudgingly promised her a tract of land on which to build a school and a church. Now Mary's friends at Creek Town, both missionaries and natives, were sure she was about to paddle to her death, along with King Eyo's finest paddlers.

A week of steady rain had turned the countryside into a sea of mud. As Mary made her way to the canoe, she slipped in the mud at the edge of the river. One of the new converts rushed to her aid. "I will pray for you every day, but I don't know if it will do any good. You are going to your death," he said as he helped Mary to her feet. There was a murmur from the crowd, and as Mary looked from the face of one person to the next, she knew they all felt the same way as the new convert.

Suddenly the Reverend Goldie yelled above the pounding rain, "It's not right for Miss Slessor to go alone. Who would be willing to accompany her to her new home?"

Mr. Bishop, the mission's printer, stepped forward. "I'm willing to accompany her," he yelled, and to prove it, he stepped into the canoe just as he was, without a scrap of luggage. "Here," he said to one of the paddlers, "hand me the children. It's time to get going."

Mary could not have agreed more. The gloomy mood of the people matched with the gloomy morning was more than she could bear. "Yes, it's time to go," she reiterated, helping Okin, Ekim, and Janie into the canoe and then passing her latest two adopted toddlers to Mr. Bishop. Within a few minutes, the five children were all arranged safely in the canoe, and Mr. Bishop helped Mary settle under the small thatched roof in the center of King Eyo's enormous canoe. Mary was covered with mud from head to toe and shivering from the cold.

The drummers began their rhythmic beat, and the canoe pulled away from the shore. There were no shouts of farewell from the crowd. The hundred or so people who had gathered stood sadly and watched their white ma disappear around the bend in the river. Mary was glad to be on her way. She turned to Mr. Bishop and said, "Thank you for coming with me. Would you like some tea?"

"That sounds like a wonderful idea," he replied.

Mary lit a small paraffin stove and placed a kettle of water on it. As she waited for the water to boil, she sliced some of her homemade bread. As they sipped tea and ate bread, Mr. Bishop began to ask about the assignment he had volunteered for. "Where exactly are we going, Miss Slessor?"

"To Ekenge," replied Mary, her excitement building. "The village is four miles inland from the river, so we'll have to leave the canoe and walk in."

Mr. Bishop, still looking a little stunned that he'd volunteered for the mission, nodded, and the two of them sat silently for some time listening to the sounds of the jungle and the splashing of the paddles in the water. A head wind was blowing, and it took a full day of paddling to get to the clearing on the riverbank, where they would leave the canoe. Darkness was beginning to descend as the paddlers pulled the canoe onto the riverbank.

"There's not much light left," said Mary, surprised by how much extra time battling the head wind had added to the trip.

Mr. Bishop stood up and stretched his long legs. "Well, we had better not waste any time then," he said. "What do you suggest?"

"I must get the children dried off and give them something to eat as soon as possible," Mary said.

"Tomorrow is Sunday, so we'll have to get everything moved up to Ekenge before midnight. We can't have anyone working on the Sabbath, can we? I'll walk on with the children. You come next with a couple of the paddlers. Bring some boxes of food and dry clothing with you. The rest of the paddlers can follow with the other boxes."

"Sounds like a good idea," agreed Mr. Bishop. "Is the trail well marked?"

"Not really," replied Mary apologetically, "but some of the paddlers know the way, and you'll have a lantern. You should be able to find your way."

Mary gathered the children around her. She gave the two older boys a small box to carry, while Janie had a kettle and two pots tied together on a piece of rope around her neck. The other two girls were so small that Mary had to carry them, one under her arm and the other on her shoulders. Mary juggled a lantern in her free hand. "We'll see you in Ekenge," she called, sounding a good deal braver than she really felt.

"God go with you," said Mr. Bishop as he helped unload a door frame and two window frames from the stern of the canoe.

Mary had walked the trail before, when she had come to negotiate permission to stay in Ekenge, but she had never traveled it at night or in the rain with two children clinging to her and three others crying and complaining. As she walked, she dared not think about the dangers ahead. She knew that if she let such thoughts creep into her mind, she'd probably turn around and walk back to the canoe. So many things could go wrong. The tribe could be on the warpath, in which case she and the children and the Creek Town canoe paddlers would be the enemy. Or the chief could be drunk or have "forgotten" that he'd promised her land for a school and a church and a house. And then there were leopards and snakes and other wild animals that could attack at any moment.

Finally, after three tense hours of slipping and sliding along the muddy path, Mary and the children reached Ekenge. Mary stood in the clearing and looked around, motioning for the children to be quiet. Something was wrong. There were no fires, no noise from the huts, no children running around. She yelled, "We have come back." There was no response. The village appeared to be deserted. Had there been a raiding party? Mary wasn't sure. Then suddenly in the darkness she heard a shuffle, and then two sleepy slaves stepped out of a hut.

"Hello," said Mary. "Where is everyone? Is there trouble?"

For a moment she forgot the slaves could not understand Efik but spoke the Bantu language, which she did not know. She used hand gestures to communicate. From the slaves' gestures, Mary guessed that the chief's mother had died earlier in the day and the village of Ekenge had gone to the funeral, leaving only a few slaves to guard the huts and gardens.

The Reverend Goldie had told Mary about some of the funeral customs in the Okoyong region which for the most part involved everyone from the tiniest baby to the most wizened old person getting drunk and performing witchcraft rituals. Sometimes events could stretch on for days.

One of the slaves led Mary to what looked like an abandoned hut. The hut had no windows, only a gaping hole for a door. Mary stepped inside and immediately noticed rainwater running down the inside of the walls and across the floor. The thatched roof was also dripping. Mary promised herself she would have a new roof made for it first thing on Monday. For now, she had to concentrate on getting the children dry, fed, and off to sleep. Another slave brought some dry sticks for a fire. Mary placed the kettle Janie had been carrying under one of the larger drips. In no time, she had a fire lit and had collected enough water to make some tea. But no matter how hard she tried, Mary could not get the children warmed up. The children sat naked, shivering in front of the feeble fire. Mary worried about them. If they didn't get some warm, dry clothes soon, they might get sick, and sickness was so often followed by death in the African jungle.

Mary poked the children's wet clothes between the thatched palm leaves in the roof in a futile attempt to stop the drips. Then she sat down and tried to sing the children to sleep. "Do not be afraid, little children, God is watching over you," she crooned, as much to herself as to them. Eventually, the children's heads dropped as they fell asleep.

Once the children were sound asleep, Mary thought about herself for the first time. She was soaked to the skin, and her feet were swollen in her boots. She pulled the boots off and set them by the fire, not thinking for a moment that it would be six weeks before she would be able to fit them back on her feet!

Half an hour later, Mr. Bishop emerged from the bush. He was covered in mud, and his face was bleeding from where he had walked into an overhanging branch. "I couldn't get the paddlers to budge," he said. "I brought what I could. I have some dry clothes for the children." He handed Mary a box of clothing. "The men said they were too tired and would not go into the jungle in the dark. It's the people of the Okoyong region, you know—they're scared enough of them in daylight."

Mary sighed deeply. She was totally exhausted, but she needed the supplies, especially the food, and she would not allow the men to work on the Sabbath. She took the box of clothing over to the fire and rummaged through it for some dry clothes for the children. Then she quickly woke each child and dressed them all before laying them gently down again to sleep. When all five children had been dressed in dry clothes, Mary sat down by the fire and started to pull her boots on. No matter how much she tugged and twisted, the boots would not go back on her swollen feet. Undaunted, she turned to Mr. Bishop and said, "The water has boiled for tea, and the tea is in one of the boxes back at the canoe. I will go and get it myself."

"You mustn't, it's not safe," pleaded Mr. Bishop. "And besides, your feet will be ripped to pieces…."

Mr. Bishop's words trailed off as Mary took the lantern and headed into the jungle. Mary sang loudly as she walked, trying not to imagine what might have caused a flock of birds to scatter from the top of a tree high above or what the crackling sound was farther along the path. When she finally reached the river, she was not surprised to see that the canoe had been pushed into the water, where it was anchored about ten feet out. She knew the men would have done this to make it more difficult for the Okoyong warriors to attack them and to keep leopards from pouncing on them. A canvas tarpaulin had been pulled over the top of the canoe, and Mary guessed the paddlers were soundly asleep underneath it.

Mary stood for a moment unsure of what to do next. She had come this far and refused go back empty-handed. Ignoring the threat of crocodiles, she stepped into the water. Her skirt billowed around her waist. She was up to her armpits in water before she reached the canoe. She pounded on the canoe with her fist, yelling at the men to wake up. Then she found a spot where the cover was not tied down, and she whipped it back, yelling some more.

"Okoyong," screamed one of the startled men. Instantly, the whole crew was awake, groping for their weapons.

Mary managed to calm them before they did her any harm, and with a few well-chosen words, she shamed them into jumping overboard and hauling the canoe ashore. By now the moon was hidden behind a bank of clouds, and the sky was pitch black. Somehow the five-foot tall, fire-haired woman from Dundee managed to cajole the paddlers into trekking four miles through enemy territory in the dark carrying her boxes.

Mary and the paddlers arrived at Ekenge just before midnight. Mr. Bishop was sitting beside the puny fire waiting for Mary. He was amazed to see all the men with her. "How did you get the men to work?" he demanded. "I tried everything I could think of and decided it was impossible!"

Mary smiled wearily and opened one of the boxes that had a change of clothes inside. Then she bid everyone good night and, totally exhausted from stumbling and clawing her way through the jungle, went into the hut to be with her children.

Mary awoke the next morning to the sound of steady rain on the thatched roof. She was too stiff to roll over. Her feet throbbed with pain, and her legs and arms were a mass of cuts and bruises. Then Mary remembered what day it was—Sunday. But not just any Sunday. It was Sunday, August 5, 1888, twelve years to the day since she had set sail from Liverpool to be a missionary in Calabar. She had left Scotland with a dream and had fought for twelve long, hard years to make it come true. Today was a day of victory. She was in Ekenge, a village in the Okoyong territory, her new home. Yet she was too tired and too sore to celebrate.

Mary could not lie in bed for long, though. There were children to dress and feed and a Sunday service to hold. It was a simple service, attended by Mr. Bishop, the paddlers from the canoe, and the few slaves left in the village. The men sang two hymns, and Mary, sitting on a box because standing was too painful, talked to them about God's love. She knew, of course, that the slaves could not understand what she said, but she hoped they would enjoy the singing.

The next day, Monday, Mary convinced the paddlers to bring the rest of her luggage from the canoe, since she could not do it herself with her swollen, cut feet. Indeed, she could barely shuffle around the hut on them. One piece of luggage still to be brought from the canoe was a small portable organ the missionaries in Duke Town had given her. Once it arrived and was placed in her hut, there was no room for her to walk around. And when she looked up at the still dripping roof, she resolved that as soon as Chief Edem, leader of Ekenge, got back from the funeral she would ask him to start building the house and school he had promised her.

It was Tuesday morning before all of Mary's things had been carried down the slippery trail to Ekenge. Once everything arrived, Mr. Bishop and King Eyo's paddlers began the journey back downriver. As Mary watched the relieved paddlers disappear into the bush, she felt more alone than ever before in her entire life. She saw clearly the challenges that lay ahead of her: the constant rain, the threat of sickness, the bloody and brutal customs and superstitions, the lack of respect the people of the Okoyong region had for life itself. As Mary stood there, she found herself praying that God would protect her and the children, at least long enough to show the tribe there was a better way to live.

Chapter 13

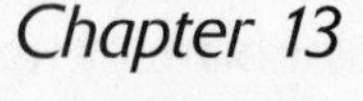

Deserting the Old Customs

The members of the tribe straggled back into Ekenge a few at a time. No one seemed particularly pleased that Mary had arrived, and when Mary spoke to Chief Edem about her need for a larger hut, he begrudgingly gave her one in his yard. The hut was filthy, and it took Mary several days to scrub it and whitewash the walls. Mary had one helper besides her children. The helper's name was Ekpa, a twelve-year-old Okoyong boy. Mary hadn't asked for his help; Ekpa just showed up. He worked alongside Mary all day, cleaning and cooking. He even helped knock holes in the wall to fit the window and door frames Mary had brought with her from Creek Town. As they worked together, Mary began to pick up the Bantu language from Ekpa. She also began to wonder whether Ekpa might become her first convert in Ekenge.

A week after moving into her new hut, Mary heard laughter and chanting coming from the village meeting area. Curious to see what was going on, she left the children in the hut and walked over to where the people had gathered. She could see a pot of liquid boiling over an open fire, and she assumed the people must be going to have some kind of special meal together. As she watched, a village elder stepped forward and spoke a few words. Mary wished she could understand what he was saying. Was he giving some kind of thanks for the food? If he was, his voice sounded particularly harsh. As he spoke, she noticed Ekpa standing at the front of the crowd flanked by two big men.

Then everything happened so quickly. The elder reached down, picked up a ladle, and scooped out some of the hot, glistening liquid, which Mary could tell was boiling oil. Mary watched in horror as Ekpa was dragged over to the elder. Suddenly she realized what was about to happen. She yelled and pushed her way through the crowd, but it was too late. The boiling oil had been poured over Ekpa's hands and arms, and Ekpa lay on the dusty ground screaming in agony.

Mary's white freckled face immediately turned bright red. She was furious. She spun around and screamed at the elder in Efik. By the way the elder spat in her face, she knew he had understood her. Then she ordered the two men to carry Ekpa to her hut. The elder translated her command as Mary led the way to her hut. There was not much Mary could do for Ekpa except dose him with laudanum and dress his wounds. As she treated him she prayed, hoping he wouldn't lose the use of his hands through infection. She wondered whether Ekpa's punishment had something to do with his helping her. In the pit of her stomach, she had a sickening feeling it did.

Mary didn't know it, but one woman had been impressed by her courageous attempt to rescue Ekpa. The woman, Ma Eme, was the sister of Chief Edem. The day after the boiling oil incident, Ma Eme came to Mary's hut. "Come sit at the back of the hut with me," she whispered in Efik, gesturing with her head at the same time.

Mary nodded and followed the large woman. Together they squatted in the dirt at the back of the hut.

"It's dangerous for us to be seen alone," whispered Ma Eme, "but I want to tell you I welcome you here. I will do what I can to help you. However, if anyone finds out I am your friend, we will both be killed. Do you understand?" Her voice was suddenly urgent.

"Yes," replied Mary. "Is that why Ekpa was burned? For being my friend?"

Ma Eme nodded. "It was said he spent too much time with you, and when he did not go on a raiding party with the other young men, he was accused of deserting the ancient customs of our people."

Mary had guessed right, but it was still a shock to hear that someone had been deliberately hurt just for helping her clean up her hut. She looked at Ma Eme, who, she thought, must be putting herself in danger, too. "Why are you doing this?" she asked.

Ma Eme looked around nervously before speaking. "The other wives are in the garden. I will tell you." She took a deep breath before going on. "I have tired of the old ways. Once I was happy with them. I was the first wife of an important chief. I had many servants, and my husband was good to me. Sometimes he hit me and bit me." She pointed to a deep scar on her left arm and then shrugged. "But he bit the other wives, too. And after all, we are just women!"

Ma Eme was silent for a moment, and Mary prodded her on. "What changed things? What made you sick of the old customs?"

Ma Eme's big brown eyes widened. "It was the funeral, the funeral of my husband. When he died, all of the wives were naturally under suspicion. It was decided that one of us must have killed him. The witch doctor was sent to find out who it was. He made all the wives stand in a circle, and then he chopped the head off a chicken and threw the chicken into the middle of the circle. It was horrible, horrible."

Mary listened carefully as Ma Eme continued her story. "We all waited. Whoever was nearest to the headless chicken when it stopped running would be the one the witch doctor accused of murdering the chief. The chicken was near me when it finally stopped, but it was a little closer to one of the new wives. She was declared a murderer and dragged off to have her arms and legs broken and be thrown into my husband's open grave. I fainted, and they left me there with the dead chicken."

Mary let out a deep sigh. "What happened then?" she asked.

"I came to live with my brother, and he is good to me. I am able to walk around the village freely. I will come again to visit when I can."

For such a big woman, Ma Eme got to her feet with surprising speed and ease. "Now I must go. I have stayed too long already. Watch yourself," she whispered to Mary.

After Ma Eme left, Mary squatted at the rear of her hut for a long time, her back resting against the warm mud-caked wall. She thanked God for sending a friend like Ma Eme, and she wondered how she would ever make progress in the village if their being friends meant risking torture or even death.

Finally, Janie broke into Mary's thoughts with news that Ekpa had awakened and was asking for food. This was a good sign, and Mary hurried off to get the sweet potato she'd saved for him.

True to her word, Ma Eme came nearly every day to talk with Mary. After a couple of weeks, some of the other women grew enough used to Mary's presence that they began hanging around Mary's hut to see what she was doing. They were especially fascinated by the portable organ and Mary's sewing machine, though they resisted Mary's attempts to sew some clothes for them. Just weeks before, seven men in a village downriver had been killed for wearing clothes. Once again, their deaths were attributed to deserting the old customs.

Although living in Ekenge was very different for Mary, some things were the same as they had been in Creek Town and Duke Town, such as the never ending stream of people who needed medical attention. Every day Mary nursed ten or twenty people with all manner of ailments. Indeed, it was treating the sick that indirectly led to her first disagreement with Chief Edem.

The conflict began one day when a runner arrived from a village about an eight-hour walk from Ekenge. The runner presented Mary with four brass rods (which the locals used as a form of money), a bottle of gin, and an urgent request. A woman visiting the man's village had told everyone about the white ma who lived at Ekenge and could cure illness. She had told them that Mary had cured her dying grandson who had been brought to her from a nearby village. This was important information for the village because their chief was gravely ill and would probably not live longer than a day or two. The runner had come to ask Mary to accompany him back to the village to cure the chief.

Mary did not know what to do. Her new patient was a chief, and if he died—or was already dead when they returned to the village—serious trouble could come of it. There would be many deaths and wild, drunken parties and Mary would be caught in the middle of it all. She might even be blamed for the chief's death. On the other hand, she had never refused to help a person who asked. Mary visited Chief Edem and Ma Eme to ask them what to do.

"You must not go," said the chief. "My power to protect you only extends an hour's walk in each direction from this village. You would be on your own, and if the chief dies, you will be blamed. Besides, it is the rainy season; the trails are flooded, and large trees have fallen in the forest. You would never make it through."

"Not only that," added Ma Eme, "if the chief dies, their village will come and pay us back for sending you to them. We could all be dead before this matter is over."

Although she respected their advice, Mary was beginning to feel like she should go. "What if it were you, Chief Edem?" she asked. "Wouldn't you want me to come and help you?"

The chief shrugged and repeated his warning. "Do not go."

That night Mary tossed and turned as she wrestled with what to do. Someone had come to ask her for help, but if she went, she could be putting the entire village of Ekenge in danger. But by the time a scrawny rooster began crowing at the first rays of sunlight peaking over the horizon, she had made up her mind. She would go and treat the ailing chief.

Mary knew that Chief Edem would not be pleased, and the chief showed his displeasure as she announced her decision. Still, short of having her killed, there was nothing he could do to stop her. Mary left instructions for the care of her children and followed the runner westward into the jungle.

Mary prayed as she walked. She was concerned about the sick chief and about getting to him in time. She was also concerned about the ordeal of getting to the village: having to avoid the potentially deadly leopards, crocodiles, and snakes, not to mention having to cross numerous tribal boundaries. Also, it had been raining for days, and the normally trickling streams they needed to cross had been transformed into raging torrents.

The rain continued to pour down, making even walking increasingly difficult. Mary's lace-up boots stuck in the mud, and it took tremendous effort to pull them free with each step. After two hours of struggling on like this, Mary signaled for the runner to stop. It was time to get practical! She took off her boots and stockings, and the runner offered to carry them for her. Then she inspected the hems of her brown woolen dress and her frilly white outer petticoat. Both were caked in mud. As Mary lifted them, she decided they must each contain five or six pounds of mud. She took them off, too, leaving her standing in the middle of the African jungle wearing only a calico slip that went from her neck to her knees, revealing her legs and bare arms, something that would have been scandalous in public back in Scotland.

"Now that feels better," Mary said to the runner.

Mary and the runner continued walking, with Mary keeping up much better now that she had fewer clothes to weigh her down. They passed through several villages, where the people simply stood in shock and stared at the red-haired white woman dressed in a calico slip.

By the time Mary and the runner arrived at the village late in the afternoon, it had stopped raining, and shafts of golden sunlight had pierced the billowing mat of clouds above. Crowds of armed men stood around the chief's hut while the women huddled in small groups and wept softly. Mary wondered whether they were weeping for the chief or over the fact that his death would mean their death as well.

Mary was escorted into the chief's hut, a smoky room with a pile of human skulls arranged neatly in the far corner. "May I have a lantern, please," she asked. One was instantly produced for her. Mary stepped forward to examine the chief, who was very weak and seemed to have some kind of stomach problem. Mary took some medicine from her bag and mixed it with water. "Drink this," she told the chief, "and then I will pray for you."

Mary ordered one of the women to make some yam soup, and when it arrived, she spooned a few drops of it into the chief's mouth. She guessed that the chief had not eaten for days, probably because no one wanted to be the last person to feed him before he died. That would make the person an obvious suspect for poisoning the chief. Mary fed the chief through the night, a drop or two at a time. By the time the sun had risen, the chief seemed a little better.

The chief continued to improve throughout the day, and that night, after conducting a Christian service, Mary fell into a fitful sleep. On the third day, she felt confident that the chief would recover fully. When she announced the news to the village, the women began to sob. They rushed up to her and knelt down, their heads touching the damp ground.

"You have saved our lives," they said, grabbing at her feet. "If you had not come, we would all have perished with our chief. How can we thank you? You will always be our mother, and we will be your children."

The journey back to Ekenge was very different from the journey to the village. About forty people from the village insisted on escorting Mary the entire way. They sang and made up poems about their white ma as they walked, and in every village they passed through, they stopped to tell of Mary's care for their chief. Mary had never liked being made a fuss of, but she knew she had made new friends along the trail, and out here in the African jungle she needed all the friends she could get.

Chapter 14

Eka Kpukpru Owo

Mary returned to Ekenge, and Chief Edem seemed pleased that she was safe. No doubt, she decided, it gave him prestige in the surrounding area to have a missionary who knew about medicine living in his village. However, much to her dismay, it didn't give Mary enough clout to get anyone to build the mission compound she had been promised before moving to the village. Mary often asked Chief Edem if he would order work to begin on her new hut and school, but the chief always gave the same answer: "Have patience; it is not building season yet." Mary wasn't at all sure that there was such a thing as building season! She wondered why the men of the village who spent hours each day lying around drunk couldn't be ordered to work on the project. Still, since she knew better than to force the point, she busied herself in other ways.

From the time Mary arrived in Ekenge, people asked her when she would begin teaching "Book"—their way of referring to reading and writing. Now, in late 1888, Mary felt that the medical needs of the village were sufficiently under control that she could concentrate on teaching the people. Chief Edem gave her his permission to begin. Virtually everyone in the village, including Chief Edem, Ma Eme, nobles, slaves, children, and dogs, showed up for the first school lesson. Excitement ran high, though no one could really grasp the meaning of reading and writing. No one in the village had much of an idea of what reading was, except that it involved speaking to a piece of paper. The people had observed Mary doing this for long periods at a time, and now they all wanted to be able to do the same.

Within a couple of weeks, most of the people had dropped out of the class. Learning to read was just too much work for them. Since they had expected to be able to read fluently after just a few lessons, most of the men went back to drinking and lying around all day. This left Mary to teach a handful of slave children who had been ordered by their masters to continue classes. Despite the falloff in numbers attending lessons, Mary wasn't discouraged. The children she was left with were intelligent and appreciated the hour or so a day they spent in school away from their chores.

About the same time that she started to teach reading and writing, Mary made contact with the neighboring village of Ifako, about a thirty-minute walk along a rough, muddy track. When the chief there had learned that Mary was teaching the people of Ekenge "Book," he had invited her to teach his people as well. Mary accepted his offer, regularly trekking to Ifako. Of course, by now she had long since given up wearing boots, preferring to trudge barefoot along the muddy jungle trails. As a result, the soles of her feet had become as tough as leather.

Mary had great success with the Bible studies she began holding in the evenings in the villages. Everyone loved the old English and Scottish hymns she had translated into their language. Mary played the organ while the children played drums and tambourines. What these tribal singers lacked in carrying an English tune they made up for in sheer volume and enthusiasm!

In Ekenge, one night after Bible study, Mary heard a lot of noise around the palaver hut, where special councils were held. She wondered what was happening. Since she knew about most of the social events that went on in the village, she decided to investigate. As she got closer to the noise, she could see that almost the whole village had gathered around in a circle. The villagers were in a frenzy, yelling and screaming. The beating of drums throbbed in her ears and the smoke from reed torches burned her nostrils as Mary stood at the back of the crowd.

Suddenly a scream pierced the air. A feeling of dread swept over Mary—was this another one of their cruel punishments? Mary pushed her way to the front of the crowd, where she saw a young woman lying naked on the ground, her hands and feet tied to stakes. Beside the woman was a large pot of boiling oil, with a warrior in a jaguar costume dancing around it. Instantly, Mary knew what was about to happen. The woman on the ground was about to have boiling oil ladled over her. Without stopping to think it through, Mary ran and stood between the warrior and the woman. Instantly, the drumming stopped, and the laugher and cheering subsided. All eyes were focused on the petite redhead who was interfering in a matter of tribal justice.

Mary glared at the warrior holding a ladle filled with hot oil. For a moment, the warrior stood with a look of confusion on his face. Then with a warlike yell, he began dancing menacingly towards Mary. For an instant, Mary was again the young woman in the backstreets of Dundee with the bully swinging his sharpened piece of metal at her. Just as she had then, she knew she could not back down; the warrior must not see any fear in her face. Mary prayed silently as the warrior came closer, the hot oil gleaming ominously in the bowl of the ladle. Except for the shuffling of the warrior's feet and the swish of the ladle, everything was totally quiet.

Finally, the moment came when Mary and the warrior stood face to face. They could not get any closer to each other. Either the warrior would hit Mary with the ladle of oil, or he would have to back away. He stared at Mary, and Mary stared back at him. Then, with a cry of disgust, the warrior threw the ladle on the ground and stepped away from Mary.

A collective gasp rose from the crowd. The white ma had stood up to a warrior, and the warrior had backed down! Chaos erupted. Everyone began talking at once. It was the most amazing scene the crowd had ever witnessed. In the midst of the confusion, the warrior scuttled away, and Mary turned to Chief Edem to plead for the woman's life. The chief would not answer Mary. Mary had stood against their customs and won! Sensing that no one would stop her, Mary bent down and untied the woman and helped her to her feet. The crowd parted, and Mary escorted the woman back to the mud hut.

The woman suffered more from shock than from anything else. In fact, the whole village was in shock for days. How, the villagers asked, could a white woman defy the power of their customs? Was her religion more powerful than theirs? Both religions believed in an all-powerful, all-knowing creator. The Africans called him *Abassi*. But they believed that Abassi wanted them to do cruel things and to be governed by superstition and magic. Now they wondered whether they might be mistaken, that perhaps Abassi was more like the God Mary described, not only all powerful but also good and kind. The thought captivated the whole tribe. Men and women, slaves and freemen, debated the question endlessly while the story of what Mary had done was passed from village to village.

Mary did not know it at the time, but this incident would be the first of many in which she would stand up to the spiritual powers of the local Africans. It was also this incident that began a legend in Calabar, the legend of Eka Kpukpru Owo, the Mother of Us All.

The woman Mary rescued was eventually allowed to return to her husband. She had been sentenced to have boiling oil poured on her stomach because she had given a chunk of yam to a man who was not her husband. In Ekenge, it was considered a crime for a woman to share food with anyone other than her husband.

Mary hoped that the incident would be a turning point for the village. She hoped it would help to get rid of many of the harsh laws and cruel superstitions. But change came slowly, with many disappointments and setbacks. One such disappointment occurred only days after Mary had rescued the woman from the hot oil.

Chief Edem became sick and sent for Mary. He was lying facedown in bed. Mary could smell the familiar rotten odor and knew what the problem was before she'd even had a chance to examine him. Sure enough, on Chief Edem's back was a huge swollen abscess. It was dark and tight around the edges. When Mary reached out and gently touched it, the chief flinched in pain. Mary said a silent prayer. A sick chief was a serious matter. Not just his life but also the lives of the whole village were at stake.

After examining the putrid wound, Mary decided that a warm poultice would be the best thing to put on it. She hoped that the mixture of herbs and lotions would draw out the poison from the abscess. The approach did not work, however. As Chief Edem's condition grew worse, Mary grew desperate. But she was not a doctor, and she couldn't think of anything else to do for him.

After two days of agony, King Edem eventually threw Mary out of his hut and called for the village witch doctor. Mary sat outside and prayed while the witch doctor busied himself inside with the chief. The witch doctor emerged an hour or so later with a triumphant look on his face. He grinned toothlessly at Mary and then spat out, "Ha, you know nothing about sickness. It is no wonder the chief is sick. Look at the things I drew out of his body!"

The witch doctor squatted beside Mary and unfolded a filthy piece of cloth. Inside were some crushed eggshells, several nails, a pouch of gunpowder, and some lead shot. Mary would have laughed out loud, except she knew that the witch doctor had the power to convince everyone in the village that the things in the cloth had actually been floating around inside the chief's body.

"It is the women," said the witchdoctor slyly. "The women have made spells and put these things inside the chief. So Chief Edem has told me to find the women who are responsible and chain them up in his yard."

Once again Mary felt helpless against such evil superstitions. The witch doctor could say whatever he liked, accuse any woman he wanted of causing the chief's sickness, and the women would be put to death by way of the poison bean. This was the standard way of deciding who was guilty of witchcraft in Calabar. The deadly esere bean was ground up, mixed with water, and made into a drink. Anyone suspected of a crime involving witchcraft was forced to swallow the drink. Occasionally someone would vomit the drink up before it hit the person's stomach and the person would live, but ninety-nine of every one hundred people who were forced to drink the crushed esere bean concoction died. Since the witch doctor told the local people that the bean drink would kill only a person who was guilty of the crime, each death confirmed the person's guilt.

Mary moved among the thirty or so women chained up in the chief's yard, praying with them and trying to encourage them. The women needed food, but the punishment for feeding a prisoner was death. Mary sat into the night with the women, hoping that perhaps the guards would go off and get drunk, giving her an opportunity to smuggle some food to the prisoners. But because the situation was too serious, the guards never once left their post. Around 2 A.M., the chief's condition worsened, and the witch doctor came to dispense some more of his "medicine," after which he produced a new crop of objects supposedly from Chief Edem's wound. This time the collection included several feathers and some small rib bones. As a result, more women were rounded up and held in chains in the chief's yard.

At daybreak, Mary walked into Chief Edem's hut and begged him to release the women in his yard. The chief, who had not slept a wink all night because of the searing pain of the abscess on his back, became enraged with Mary. How dare she interfere in the ways of the tribe? For all he knew, the gods could be punishing him for ever allowing her into the village. Mary bravely told him once again about God's love, but this too enraged him until he ordered his guards to move him and all of the women in the yard to one of his outlying farms. The chief ordered Mary not to follow.

By lunch time, the yard was empty and silent. The chief and the women had all left. Mary could do nothing but wait and pray. A day went by, and more women in the village were rounded up and dragged off wailing and sobbing to the chief's farm. Another day passed, and then Ma Eme slipped into Mary's hut and whispered the wonderful news—Chief Edem was recovering! There was just one problem. The chief had already condemned many of the women prisoners to death. Mary became frantic. There had to be a way to save the women, and she had to think of one quickly. She sensed that Ma Eme wanted to see the women go free as well. Suddenly it came to her. They had to convince the chief that the greatest thing he could do would be to free all of the women. Mary thought she knew how to do that. She turned to Ma Eme, her eyes bright and urgent. "You must go back to your brother and tell him that many people will respect him if he lets all the women go. It will show everyone that he has greater power than they, and that he is not afraid of what the women could do to him if they are not killed."

A smile spread across Ma Eme's face. "You are very shrewd," she told Mary. "No chief wants to look like a coward. I will go."

Mary waited anxiously for Ma Eme to return. When Ma Eme did return, the women of the village were with her. The chief had let them go! Ma Eme was very proud of her achievement, though she did add that the witch doctor had insisted that one slave woman be held responsible for the chief's sickness. But, Ma Eme hastened to add with great pride, even the slave woman had not been given the poison esere bean. What Ma Eme did not add was that the woman had been sold to the Inokon tribe, known for its cannibalism, especially of slaves bought from other tribes.

Each new day at Ekenge seemed to bring some new crisis or challenge for Mary, whose fame spread throughout the district. This meant that envoys from other tribes were constantly arriving to ask her help in a medical matter or to settle some dispute. There were also times when Mary was too exhausted to continue in her work, especially after she'd spent a sleepless night in her hut. Living in chief Edem's yard with his many wives and female slaves meant that she was awakened at all hours by the chief and his drunken guests. After five months of little sleep, Mary needed a quiet place to call her own, a place where she could pray out of view of prying eyes, raise her children in peace, and permanently set up her school and little church.

A hut of her own did not seem too much to ask for, but Mary knew that the chief would not allow a place to be built for her until he was willing to welcome her permanently into the tribe. Right now she was still on trial, and after her failure to cure the chief's abscess, she wondered whether her days of living at Ekenge were numbered.

Thankfully, Chief Edem did not hold a grudge, and in January 1889, Mary awoke to the distant sound of hacking knives and axes. For some reason that she would never find out, the chief had declared it building season. At long last, Mary was about to get her own home.

Chapter 15

A Wee Bit of Help

Mary woke the children and hurried to the site on the edge of the village that was to be her new home. The area was crowded with people who tripped over each other in their eagerness to work. Mary smiled and shook her head. Would she ever understand the African mind? Yesterday she had not been able to rouse a single person to help carry water to a woman who had gone into labor and was about to give birth. Today, the whole village was united in work, whacking at tree limbs with knives and axes and digging up roots with sharpened sticks.

The people laughed and cheered when they saw Mary. As she surveyed the site, Mary realized she needed to act fast to have any say in how her new home should look. She quickly thought about what would be the most practical arrangement for her and settled on a kitchen and living hut, a girls' hut, a boys' hut, and a hut for herself. Each hut would be about thirty feet long and ten feet wide and would be laid out on the site in such a way as to form three sides of a square. This would allow her to one day build a larger house in the middle and use the huts as storage areas.

Work progressed noisily, and despite the general level of disorganization, huts began to take shape on the property. First a trench was dug where the walls of each hut were to be placed, then the men hacked down huge branches with forks in them. The branches were positioned one at each corner of the hut with the fork facing up. They were the main supports for the roof. Smaller branches were laid in the forks and lashed down with dried grasses to form a frame. More branches were laid across this frame and lashed down, and then woven mats were finally tied down on top of it all.

The walls of the huts were made in a similar way to the roof, except that instead of having woven mats lashed to the outside, the branches were plastered with thick red clay. Before the walls were mudded, a smoky fire was lit inside each new hut. Chief Edem left several of his slaves there to make sure the fire burned all night and did not get out of control and burn down the wooden frames. The chief explained that the purpose of the fire was to smoke out any insects living in the wood or thatch and to dry out the wood.

The next day the women's work of plastering the huts with clay began. Mary joined in with great enthusiasm. After they finished mudding the walls, the women began furnishing the inside of the huts. They made a clay fireplace in the kitchen. Someone was inspired to fashion a counter out of clay. The counter had special hollows in it where Mary could keep her china. Inspired by Mary's appreciation, the women made a table for Mary's sewing machine, and even a clay couch to sit on.

By the time the huts were completed, Mary was amazed at all the people of Ekenge had done for her. She had no idea it was possible to make a hut so comfortable from sticks and mud. There were even holes in the walls for windows and doors. In a letter back to her home church in Scotland, Mary asked whether anyone would be willing to come to Ekenge and install window frames and a door in the holes for her. She never really expected anyone to come all the way from Scotland to do such a thing, but she felt that it did no harm to ask.

One hot July evening in 1889, Mary sat cross-legged on the sandy ground at her new compound eating corn stew with her hands. She was surrounded by her five children and an assortment of scrawny goats and chickens that darted forward whenever one of the children dropped a scrap of food. As she ate, she thought she heard an unfamiliar sound in the jungle. She stood up and listened carefully. There it was again; it was singing—but not just any singing. It was singing with a strong Scottish accent!

Mary brushed down her skirt and smoothed back her short cropped hair. She was getting a European visitor, her first in nearly a year. A minute later, Mary heard yelling along the path and saw several Ekenge men reach for their guns. "No, no, don't shoot," she called. "It's my friend."

In fact, Mary had no idea who it was, only that he had a Scottish accent. All of a sudden a short, stocky man with a thick bushy beard and accompanied by a tall African man emerged from the jungle. Mary rushed forward to welcome them.

"Mr. Charles Ovens at your service, Miss Slessor," said the man, smiling and holding out his hand to shake hers. "I believe you need a wee bit of help with some windows and doors?"

Mary laughed out loud. Her help had arrived—all the way from Scotland. By the sound of his accent, the man was from the Dundee area. Within hours, the two were on their way to becoming great friends. Charles Ovens had brought Mary a bundle of letters and several newspapers from home. In return, Mary told him all about the lives of the Africans in the Okoyong region. Charles also learned that Mary considered the new mud huts a temporary solution to her needs. What she dreamed of was a large house situated in the square formed by the huts. The house would have a kitchen and living room downstairs and bedrooms for herself and her children upstairs. Right there and then, Charles Ovens decided he would build Mary the house.

A few days later, Charles began to draw up plans for the house and made a list of the materials he would need to order from Duke Town. As he worked away, another crisis broke out in the village, and he was able to see firsthand just how this petite woman from Dundee handled herself with the locals.

It was midafternoon, and Mary had just begun grinding manioc to make flour to be used in the evening meal. As she worked, she heard a loud thud, like something heavy falling, followed by a series of loud groans. "Charles, someone's hurt," she yelled, grabbing her medical bag and running towards the sound. Charles followed along right behind her. Mary reached a clearing where King Edem's oldest son Etim had been building himself a hut. In an instant, Mary could see what had happened. Etim had been trying to move a heavy support branch alone, and the branch had fallen, pinning him underneath it. Mary and Charles rushed to him and rolled the branch off.

"Move your legs," urged Mary. "Show me that you can move your legs."

An intense look of concentration came over Etim, but it was no use—his legs would not work.

"God help us all, he's paralyzed," muttered Mary in English for the benefit of Charles Ovens.

"Let's get him into a hut," Charles suggested, grabbing a couple of bamboo poles from a pile Etim had stacked in one corner. He pulled off his shirt and tied it to the two poles, forming a sling in the middle. "You take his arms, and I'll take his legs. On the count of three," he said. "One, two, three."

With a loud groan, Etim was lifted onto the makeshift stretcher, and Mary and Charles began dragging him to Mary's hut. The pain from the movement was too much for Etim, who lapsed into unconsciousness.

Along the way Mary changed her mind. "No, we had better get him straight to the chief. He looks like he could die any minute," she said.

Before Mary and Charles got to the chief's yard with Etim, the news was out. Terrified women stood shaking as they passed. Small children scurried away, and old men rattled the bones on their family shrines.

"Why does everyone look so afraid?" asked Charles Ovens.

"There's no such thing as an accident in African religion," Mary responded frantically. "If he dies, someone or everyone will be blamed for causing this to happen."

Chief Edem met them at the door to his hut and helped carry his son inside. Mary and Charles Ovens did what they could to make Etim comfortable, but there seemed little hope he would live long. Mary stayed with him as the hours dragged into days and the days into weeks. Sometimes Etim was conscious, and sometimes he lapsed into unconsciousness. While Mary watched over him, she had plenty of time to think. Unless a miracle took place, she was convinced he would eventually die and then there would be massive bloodshed one way or another. What could she do to stop it? It was useless telling the local people that no one had caused the accident, that accidents can happen for no good reason. That was far too strange a concept for them to accept. There had to be another way. As she watched the long procession of people who paraded through the hut to show their respects, Mary came up with an idea. She realized it might not work, but it was the best idea she had.

After two weeks, Etim was near death. Despite her best efforts, Mary had not been able to coax him to eat anything since the accident, and his breathing had become shallow and irregular. Desperate efforts were made to revive him. The witch doctor rubbed hot pepper into Etim's eyes and blew it up his nose. He propped Etim's mouth open with twigs and blew smoke into his mouth and nostrils. Mary begged him to stop the torture, but he insisted on trying to draw the departing spirit back into Etim's body. The rest of the family helped out, too. They yelled prayers to the young man's spirit, begging it not to leave, but to no avail. Etim finally died.

Mary said a brief prayer for Etim and slipped out of the hut. She called one of Ma Eme's slaves, gave him a letter, and told him not to stop until he had delivered it to the missionaries at Duke Town. Mary was sure Ma Eme would approve of her "borrowing" a slave in a crisis like this.

By the time Mary got back to her compound to tell Charles Ovens the bad news, he had already guessed it. The village was in an uproar with wailing and yelling everywhere. People were running aimlessly in all directions, and the men were carrying their spears, ready to avenge the death of the chief's son.

Mary had anticipated the next move. The witch doctor was called to announce just who was responsible for the death of Etim. It took him only a few minutes of manipulating skull bones, blowing smoke, and examining Etim's fingernails to be certain. He stood in the chief's yard to make his announcement. "It is the people of Kuri who have killed this young man. Their spirits came in the night and waited to ambush him in the forest. We must avenge his death."

Mary watched in horror as the men of the village raised their spears into the air and danced wildly in circles. The men kept it up until one of Chief Edem's brothers arrived to lead them off down the trail to raid the village of Kuri.

Mary hurried back to Etim's body, praying that the men would bring their captives back alive rather than killing them on the spot. Once again she realized how fickle the African view of cause and effect was. Next week a war party from another village could come and raid Ekenge because one of their men had slipped and fallen and died on a trail somewhere.

As she hurried along, Mary carried with her a pair of men's pinstriped pants and a jacket that she had received in a box of clothes sent to her from Dundee. She also carried about twelve yards of green and yellow silk, which she had been saving to make dresses for the children. She hoped it would serve to make Etim look important, so important that the people of Ekenge would allow his spirit to enter the otherworld alone, without the spirits of those who would soon have to be killed to accompany him.

Inside the hut, Mary propped Etim's body up against the wall and began to dress him. First she pulled on the pants and then the jacket. She wound the colorful silk around his chest and abdomen. Then she asked one of the chief's slaves to fetch her some red and white paint, which she dabbed over Etim's face in a circular pattern, trying to make him look regal. Finally, she pushed some cheap rings onto his fingers and popped a brown hat with peacock feathers pinned on it onto his head.

"Come and help me," she yelled out the door of the hut.

Several men appeared.

"We must pay homage to a great man like Etim," she announced. "Ask the chief for his chair and put it in the women's yard. We must place Etim on it so everyone can see how splendid he looks."

The men nodded and hurried off to do as the white ma had instructed. An hour later, Etim's fully dressed corpse, except for shoes, was perched on the chief's chair in the women's yard. Chief Edem's slaves took turns holding an umbrella over the body to keep it shaded. Mary placed a silver-handled whip in Etim's right hand and propped a mirror in his left so that he could admire himself in the afterlife.

It was a strange sight to see the young black man's body decked out in clothes for the first time. About twenty women, most holding babies or small children, sat nearby chanting songs designed to guide Etim's spirit to a safe resting place.

No sooner had Mary finished "honoring" the corpse than the war party arrived back from Kuri, bringing twelve prisoners with them. Two women and three children were among the prisoners; the rest were young men about the same age as Etim.

Mary could see the terror in the prisoners' eyes, and she knew it was well founded. Unless her plan worked, these prisoners from Kuri would be killed and thrown into the grave with Etim.

The village was in no hurry to bury Etim. There was much partying to be done before that would happen. Besides, the men told Mary it was good for the prisoners to suffer in this life as well as the next for killing Etim.

Mary decided right then that either she or Charles Ovens would stay with the prisoners every moment until the funeral was over. By doing so, she and Charles at least had some chance of preventing the prisoners from being killed. Mary took the night shift, willing herself to stay awake for three nights while the people of the village became increasingly drunk and wild. When Charles Ovens was not watching over the prisoners, he spent his time making a magnificent coffin for Etim.

Finally, after four days, Etim's body, which had been the central decoration of the partying, began to smell in the humid African heat. Everyone agreed it was time to bury Etim. As the witch doctor and the three warriors guarding the prisoners made their plans, Mary moved in closer to them, hoping to hear what the prisoners' fate would be.

"I have ground three handfuls," said the witch doctor.

"So, it's to be death by poison beans," Mary mumbled under her breath.

The witch doctor looked over the prisoners. "Unchain this one," he said pointing to one of the women.

Obediently one of the guards unlocked the woman's chain, but the woman was too scared to move and had to be dragged into Chief Edem's hut. Mary hated to leave the other eleven prisoners, not knowing what the guards might do to them, but the situation was desperate. She crept quietly into the chief's hut. In the dim light, she could make out the witch doctor lifting a carved wooden cup to the woman prisoner's lips. "Drink, you demon, drink," he yelled as he pulled her head back.

Mary did not have a second to lose. She dashed forward and grabbed the woman's hand. "Run!" she yelled. "Run!"

The witch doctor was so shocked he dropped the wooden cup to the floor, spilling its deadly contents. In the commotion that followed, Mary and the prisoner ran out the door and escaped to Mary's new home.

Mary was thankful she had insisted that Chief Edem declare her house a safe haven and sanctuary, though she had doubts about whether he would honor his word in this case. Still, she shoved the woman through the door and hoped. "Charles, hide her quickly," she yelled, and then she raced back out the door, slamming it shut behind her.

Mary ran back to the chief's yard to try to protect the other prisoners. As she ran, she prayed that it wasn't too late, that none of the other prisoners had been forced to drink the poisonous liquid. She arrived out of breath but in time. The other eleven prisoners were still alive.

Chief Edem was furious with Mary. How dare this foreigner interfere with the customs of the village? Yet he honored his word and did not send anyone into Mary's house to retrieve the other prisoner. In the meantime, Mary stood her ground, threatening anyone who tried to take any of the other prisoners into the hut to be poisoned. The standoff dragged on for over a day. Charles Ovens marveled at Mary's calm in the midst of it. He confided in her that his own nerves were so on edge he could hardly think straight.

Finally, on the sixth day after Etim's death, the event Mary had been waiting for happened. It was early evening when a party of missionaries and native helpers from Duke Town burst into Ekenge. As Mary welcomed them loudly, she announced they had come to show their respect for Etim in a very special way. The villagers gathered around to see what would happen. Outside the palaver hut the missionaries set up a table. They opened a black leather case and took out a lantern contraption and placed it on the table. Then they draped a sheet between two palm trees.

One of the missionaries struck a match and lit the lantern. An immediate gasp of amazement went through the crowd, followed by stunned silence. The eyes of everyone in the village were on the screen. Mary heard mothers whisper to their children, "White man's magic." The missionaries had brought with them a magic lantern show. As they placed glass plates with pictures painted on them in front of the lantern, the image was projected onto the sheet hung between the two palm trees. Everyone sat cross-legged, spellbound by the images they saw—images they could never have imagined of horses pulling carriages, steam trains, and elaborate palaces.

When the show was over, Mary explained to the village that the missionaries had come to honor Etim in a new way, not with killing but with words and pictures. She desperately hoped this would convince the village that the prisoners should be set free. It worked. Begrudgingly, Chief Edem let the prisoners go, one at a time.

The next day Etim was buried in his beautiful coffin, along with his umbrella, his mirror, and a single cow that had been slaughtered to feed him in the afterlife.

It had taken every ounce of Mary's faith and effort, but Mary had achieved the impossible. For the first time in the Okoyong region, a member of a chief's family had been buried without bloodshed.

Perhaps, Mary told herself as she put her children to bed that night, she would live to see God break the chains of superstitious customs and practices in the Okoyong region.

Chapter 16

Bit by Bit

Mary almost had to pinch herself to believe that such a wonderful day had arrived. Today she and Charles Ovens were dedicating the new church at Ifako along with the missionary house and medical dispensary at Ekenge. There was much celebrating, and a number of important men from both villages gave long, complimentary speeches. Since Mary had banned rum and gin from the celebration, instead of the people sitting around getting drunk after the speeches, Mary took them all on a tour of the wonderful house Charles Ovens had built for her and the children. The people marveled at the glass panes in the windows and put their ears against the clock face to hear the ticking sound. They turned the flywheel on the sewing machine and watched the needle go up and down. They peered at themselves in the wall mirror and took turns holding Mary's china cups. Some people, even some of the bravest warriors, were reluctant to climb the stairs to the second floor. Except for perhaps climbing a tree, they had never been up so high before!

That night, after everyone had left and the children were tucked in bed, Mary and Charles Ovens sat around the fire laughing about the events of the day.

"I wish every day could be like today," said Mary wistfully, poking the dying fire. "You know, I don't even think they missed drinking; they were kept too busy. And did you see how fascinated they were with the windows and doorknobs?"

Charles nodded. "Aye, it would be a great thing if they were able to work and trade for such things themselves instead of lying around drinking."

Mary nodded in agreement, but she knew that very little trading went on between the tribes of the Okoyong region and those on the coast. What little trading did take place usually consisted of slaves sold to coastal tribes in exchange for guns, rum, gin, and chains.

As Mary lay on her clay bed that night, she began wondering how she could get the people of Ekenge to understand that they could produce palm oil and root crops to trade with the coastal tribes for useful things such as pots, mirrors, and work tools. Of course, she knew that such items were not really important to the people of Ekenge. But if she could figure out some way to get the people trading for them, two good things would follow. One, the village would be kept busy and there would be little time for the people to sit around and get drunk, and two, for the first time the people would have meaningful, nondeadly dealings with the coastal tribes.

By morning Mary had a plan. She would invite a delegation of Ekenge leaders to go with her to Creek Town, where she would introduce them to her old friend King Eyo and ask him to help set up trade links between the two tribes. Everyone in the village thought the idea was very strange. Why ever would they go into enemy territory if not to rob or kill? Mary, though, would not give up. After several weeks of Mary's pestering Chief Edem, the chief finally agreed to get a group of leaders together and go with Mary to Creek Town.

Mary arranged for Ma Eme to watch the children. The next morning she was ready to go. Mary suspected that the men were afraid to take the journey, since it would be the farthest any of them had traveled from their village. Her suspicions were quickly confirmed as she neared the riverbank. The sounds of wailing and crying filled the air. Women were clinging to their village leaders. "Don't go. We will never see you again. The gods don't want you to leave us," they begged through deep sobs.

The seven men looked sheepishly at Mary, who immediately took charge of the situation. She ordered the men to climb aboard the canoe. The canoe rocked wildly from side to side as the men took their places amid the cargo of palm nuts, maize, yams, and palm oil. Mary's face showed a tinge of doubt as she climbed in herself. The canoe was small and obviously overloaded. The men of Ekenge were warriors and farmers, not rivermen. Despite her doubts, Mary said a prayer and ordered the canoe be pushed out onto the river.

The canoe had floated about ten feet offshore when several of the men leaned to the right to wave good-bye to their families. This proved too much for the overburdened canoe, which quietly rolled over and sank. Thankfully, the water was only chest deep. Mary ordered the men to rescue the trading goods and carry them ashore.

Chief Edem carried a palm leaf basket filled with yams and threw it down at the water's edge. "I told you we should not go," he said to Mary. "The river gods are trying to kill us. It is a sign. If we try again, they will succeed, and we will all die."

"Nonsense!" retorted Mary, twisting the hem of her skirt to wring some water out of the garment. "That wasn't any river god. That was a small canoe with far too much in it. Get me a bigger canoe."

The chief opened his mouth to say more and then closed it, no doubt realizing how pointless it was to argue with Mary.

Soon a larger canoe was found, and the villagers' trading goods were loaded into it. Mary had to chase down several of the men, including Chief Edem, who had hidden behind a nearby tree. She dragged the men to the canoe, sat them down, and told them to stay put. The men did as they were told, and this time when the canoe was pushed out onto the river, it did not capsize. The men began to paddle in a rhythmic motion, and the canoe slipped away downriver.

The group had been traveling for half an hour when Mary spotted the gleam of swords between the casks of palm oil. She sighed deeply. The men had been warned not to bring weapons, but who could blame them for trying? The only reason they had ever left their territory before was to go on raiding parties. Mary thought for a moment. If she were to get angry at the men for bringing their weapons, the men would be embarrassed and might insist they turn around and go back to Ekenge. The trip was too important for that to happen. So while the men were distracted by a hippopotamus on the shore, Mary grabbed the swords and dropped them overboard into the silty water. She watched for a reaction from the men, but there was none. From the splash the weapons made, she was certain they must have guessed what she'd done. Instead, not one word was ever said about the swords. It was as if they had never existed.

The trip to Creek Town was a huge success from the start. King Eyo welcomed the men from Ekenge as if they were long lost brothers. He had feasts prepared for them and led them on a tour of his town. He also helped them barter their goods for useful items. Mary insisted that no goods would be traded for gin, rum, or guns. Mary's missionary friend Hugh Goldie invited Mary and the men to a Christian service at which King Eyo himself spoke from the Bible about the God of Peace.

The party stayed three days in Creek Town, and before they left to return to Ekenge, King Eyo and Chief Edem made solemn promises to each other. King Eyo agreed to send men upriver to trade with the people of Ekenge and Ifako. He would even lend the villagers several of his larger canoes for the times they wanted to come downriver and trade in Creek Town. In return, Chief Edem promised to put a stop to the raiding parties that plundered the farms in his region of Calabar and not to attack Efik men who traveled farther inland.

Mary had done what two years before, when she first ventured into Okoyong territory, had seemed impossible. The chiefs were now beginning to open up their territories. They were making treaties together and beginning to trust each other.

The men received an enthusiastic welcome when they arrived back in Ekenge. It was as if they had come back from the dead, and to many people in the village, they may as well have! The night was filled with singing and praying, trying on trinkets from Creek Town, and telling stories of King Eyo and his amazing house. Drummers beat out news of the new treaty with the coastal tribes. A drummed message could carry for up to seven miles, and as was the custom, it would be repeated by other drummers deeper into the jungle. Ma Eme assured

Mary that every tribe within two hundred miles of Ekenge would hear the news.

Mary enjoyed new respect among the people of the Okoyong region. Chief Edem began asking her opinion on more and more things, and chiefs from other villages sent for her to settle their disputes.

Now that King Eyo's canoes were traveling regularly between Ekenge and Creek Town, Mary used the opportunity to visit the other missionaries downriver, especially after Charles Ovens had left to help at another mission station. After he left, Mary felt truly alone for the first time. She missed singing Scottish songs and reminiscing with Charles about life back in Scotland.

A new recruit named Charles Morrison had recently joined the missionary staff in Duke Town. Charles was a serious young man of twenty-four who loved to read and write poetry and who had been sent out to teach the Africans how to be teachers themselves. Mary liked Charles Morrison from the minute she met him, and he liked her as well.

Over the next year, Mary made several trips to Duke Town to visit Charles Morrison, and Charles came to Ekenge to nurse her when she became ill with a bout of malaria. Somewhere along the way, the two of them fell in love, though Mary found it hard to believe. After all, she was old enough to be his mother! Still, by the time Mary was ready to return to Scotland at the end of 1890 for her third furlough, Charles Morrison had asked her to marry him. Mary agreed, under one condition—that he join her in Ekenge. Whatever else happened, her work among the people there must not stop.

Back in Scotland, Mary applied to the missions board for permission to marry Charles Morrison and have him move to Ekenge with her. The mission board would not agree to her request. Charles Morrison was a highly educated man who was needed in Duke Town to train teachers. If Mary wanted to marry him, she was informed that she'd have to move to Duke Town. A wife moved to her husband's work, not the other way around. This response posed a serious dilemma for Mary. Her work had always come first, and she believed it was God who had led her to Ekenge. Did she have the right to change that calling just so she could get married?

After wrestling with the question for more than a month, Mary finally concluded that she needed to stay with the African people in Ekenge. The people trusted her, and there was still a lot of work to do among them. So Mary called off the engagement.

With the engagement behind her, she threw herself into her new "project." From the time Charles Ovens had come to Ekenge, Mary had wondered why the natives couldn't be trained to be carpenters and other tradesmen. After all, the men were wonderful wood carvers. If the Africans were given the right tools and shown how to use them, they could make things for themselves. The missionaries would no longer need to beg carpenters to come all the way from Scotland to make a few door and window frames. But while it seemed a sensible and straightforward idea to Mary, it was a completely foreign notion to the missions board. As far as the board was concerned, Africans were poor and helpless and needed white people to do things for them. Did Mary really believe that tribal people were capable of learning trades? they questioned. But Mary would not take no for an answer. She spoke out about her plan whenever she could, and she wrote so many letters to the missions board that her hand ached. In the end she won. She convinced the missions board that it should recruit a tradesman with a desire to train Africans and have him set up a training school in Calabar to teach adults carpentry and other new skills.

By February 1892, Mary was ready to return to Africa for the fourth time. She dreaded seeing Charles Morrison again, although she had already written him that she had decided not to marry him.

As it turned out, Mary's decision to stay in the Okoyong region proved to be the right decision at a crucial time. In the year that Mary was in Scotland, tremendous changes were taking place in Calabar, many of which she had read about in the newspaper. Just after Mary left for Scotland, a new British consul was appointed to the Niger Coast Protectorate, of which Calabar was part. Sir Claude MacDonald, the new consul, had been given the task of bringing British law and order to the area between the Calabar and Cross Rivers. This had never been attempted before—the inland areas had always been too dangerous to enter—and the British had always stayed close to the coast.

What Mary did not know was that while she was away, Sir Claude MacDonald had been trying to decide the best way to introduce British law to the region. Whenever he asked a person for his or her opinion on the matter, the person had always the same response: "You need Mary Slessor."

"But that's not possible," Mary stammered as she stood before Sir Claude MacDonald shortly after arriving back in Calabar. "I mean, thank you for the offer, sir, but there is no way I could be made vice-consul and represent you in Ekenge. I'm a missionary, not a politician. There is already enough work out there for a hundred missionaries, and I am a lone woman. Surely you can see that."

Mary and Sir Claude talked on through the afternoon, and by early evening, the consul had managed to win Mary over. Mary had finally changed her mind when Sir Claude MacDonald told her that some white person would have to be sent into the Okoyong region to bring law and order, and if Mary would not agree to be that person, he had no choice but to send for a representative from England. The thought of a young man straight out of some English academy with no knowledge of the local language or customs being given charge of enforcing British law in the Okoyong region terrified Mary. The whole area would be in an uproar within weeks, and there would no doubt be massive bloodshed. Since Mary could not let that happen, she agreed to become vice-consul, making her the judge and jury of all matters of law in the Okoyong region. Now she would have more than ever to do.

When Mary finally made her way upriver, crowds of people were waiting to greet her. They had missed their white ma. Ma Eme was especially pleased to see Mary again and to learn of Mary's new, official title. Ma Eme did more than ever to help Mary bring peace to the area. Often she heard of trouble before Mary, and while she dared not openly warn Mary every time, she would send one of her slaves to her with a particular medicine bottle and a request for it to be filled. This was a signal to alert Mary to trouble. When she received the signal, Mary would gather her provisions and arrange for her children to be taken care of, all before the official request for her help arrived. The people were always amazed at how she "sensed" trouble, never suspecting for a moment that Ma Eme was working with her.

More often than not, Mary was called to resolve arguments between chiefs. Sometimes she had to travel for a day or so to reach them, and she would worry as she traveled that they might kill each other before she arrived. To try to head this off, she would send one of Ma Eme's slaves running through the jungle ahead of her. In the slave's hand would be a piece of paper with a blob of red wax and Mary's official vice-consul seal pressed into it. It didn't matter much what Mary wrote on the paper, since no one could read it, but the paper itself looked impressive and often kept the parties from fighting until she arrived.

To sit down and talk instead of killing each other was a new thing for the people of the Okoyong region. Mary patiently taught the people how to present their cases to her. She would sit in the shade of a kapok tree and take out her knitting. Then, as she clicked away with her knitting needles, she would ask the group on one side to state the problem and then allow the opposing group to say what it thought. This would go on and on, sometimes for thirty-six hours straight, as the chiefs repeated the same information over and over, hoping to impress Mary. Finally, when she sensed that everyone was worn out from talking, Mary would ask each side to sum up its arguments, and then she would announce her decision.

After the decision had been rendered came the part Mary hated. The chiefs of both parties would agree to Mary's ruling by cutting an oath together. To do this, the two men would clasp hands while a third slashed the back of their hands with a knife. Then this third man would sprinkle salt, pepper, and corn into the bleeding wounds. The two chiefs would then chant an oath agreeing to stick to Mary's decision, and to make it final, they would take turns licking each other's wound.

Mary could not stand to watch as the oaths were cut, but she did not forbid the practice, although she had the power to do so. She decided it was better to allow the people some of their old ways, especially ones that did no real harm to anyone.

Bit by bit Mary worked to change the cruel practices of the Okoyong region. Some changes took longer than others, but she never gave up. By 1896, there was basic law and order in place throughout the region. As a result, Mary was able to report to Sir Claude MacDonald that raiding villages to capture slaves had stopped, that there were no more human sacrifices at funerals, that few women were drunkards and many men were sober a lot of the time, too, that twins were hardly ever killed (though many were still neglected until they died), and that more often than not the mother of the twins was allowed to live. With only a Bible and incredible courage, Mary Slessor had changed the cruel customs and culture of a region. She was now forty-eight years old and had survived in Calabar for twenty years, longer than anyone could have hoped or predicted.

Many missionaries began to urge Mary to return to Duke Town to live, especially after she received news that Charles Morrison had died of an unknown disease while visiting America. Her friends also wanted her to take better care of her health and rest more, which she could do comfortably in Duke Town. But Mary had not yet finished her missionary work. The people of Ekenge still needed her, and she would not leave them. Still, even she would have been daunted had she known what lay ahead for her.

Chapter 17

One of a Kind

In 1896, Mary Slessor had to move, not because she wanted to but because just about everyone in the village of Ekenge had moved out. The villagers had come to enjoy growing crops and producing palm oil to trade with the tribes downriver. However, in the process, they exhausted the nutrients in the soil around the village, and the soil no longer produced ample harvests. The people of the village noticed that the small farms about ten miles upriver produced much bigger and healthier crops than theirs. Many of them, including Ma Eme and her household, started a new village called Akpap at a place where the soil had not been overused. The new village was closer to the Cross River, making transporting goods to the canoes for the trip downriver much easier.

Mary moved to the new village, though she kept the mission house in Ekenge and returned to it regularly to help the few families and Chief Edem who had chosen to stay behind.

Not long after she had settled in Akpap, tragedy struck the region. A disease was brought upriver by the traders. Mary groaned when she heard the symptoms: high fever followed by an itchy rash that turned into bright red lumps. It could be only one thing: smallpox. Mary did what she could. A vaccine had been developed for the disease, but it was hard to get in large quantities, and it was capable of killing the person it was given to. Still, Mary sent to Duke Town for as much of the vaccine as the people could spare. She worked harder than ever administering it to as many people as possible.

Mary raced between Akpap, Ekenge, and Ifako trying to help people, but there was little she could do. Despite the vaccine, the bodies kept piling up, first ten at a time, then twenty, then hundreds. There were too many to bury. Mary watched helplessly as some of her oldest and dearest friends died. One of them was Chief Edem, the man who had both frustrated and helped her when she first came to Ekenge. When he died, Mary sat by his body and wept. She could not stand to leave his body to be eaten by rats and other animals. As exhausted as she was, she dragged herself to the doorway of his hut and picked up a digging stick. She dug a shallow grave, which she rolled the chief's body into. She looked around the chief's hut for something he would have wanted to be buried with and chose his sword, a gun, his staff, and a whip. Then she covered his body with dirt and left the hut. There was no one left in Ekenge to mourn their dead chief.

As she walked through the abandoned village, Mary could not help but think of what the death of a chief had meant when she first arrived in Ekenge twelve years before. The drunken partying would have been under way by now, the witch doctor would have been called to announce who was responsible for the death, and the drums would be beating the news across the Okoyong region. Mary comforted herself with the fact that such practices no longer occurred. She turned away from the village and onto the path that led to Akpap. Memories of her dead friends flooded through her mind as she wearily made her way home.

Eventually the epidemic ran its course, and even though Mary did not catch smallpox herself, she was left physically and emotionally exhausted by the epidemic, so exhausted, in fact, that she did not put up her usual fiery objections when the missions board ordered her to return to Scotland for a furlough. She took four of her girls with her—fifteen-year-old Janie, five-year-old Mary, three-year-old Alice, and one-year-old Maggie. She would not think of leaving Calabar without them. Although none of them had a single "decent" piece of clothing to wear, a missionary box had recently arrived from Scotland. As a result, Mary and the children traveled to Scotland dressed in secondhand clothes donated for poor, naked Africans! Mary couldn't have cared less how she looked, which was good, because she found it difficult to wear shoes. Her feet had become wide and tough through going barefoot for so long and did not take kindly to being crammed into dainty shoes.

The furlough itself was difficult for Mary. With four black children trailing behind her, she stood out in a crowd. Often someone would recognize her, and then she would be barraged with questions. Also, the missions board had arranged huge receptions for their most famous missionary. In Glasgow, Mary stood for over an hour shaking people's hands as they left the reception. All of the fuss exhausted Mary, who longed to be back among "her" people in Calabar. The Foreign Missions Committee, on the other hand, was worried about her obvious poor health and wanted her to stay longer in Scotland. However, Mary, in her usual stubborn way, simply said to the committee, "If you don't send me back, I'll swim!" She probably meant it, too. She got her way, however, and in December 1898, she was once again on a ship bound for Calabar.

When she got back to Duke Town, Mary received a warm welcome, though not a happy one. Many sad things had occurred while she was in Scotland. When she left, the Calabar mission for the first time ever had all of its upriver stations manned by missionaries. Eight new missionary recruits had been sent out for this purpose. But six months later, five of the new missionaries were dead from disease, and two others were too ill to continue and had returned to Scotland to die. The deaths of the missionaries had brought to an end the mission's hopes of expanding farther inland. There was no way the mission could send more missionaries to certain death. Mary, however, had set her sights on the Aro tribe, the most ruthless cannibals in Calabar. But given the situation in Duke Town, she did not discuss her plans with anyone there. The people would have thought her crazy for even considering going there and would have forbidden her from going.

In December 1899, a year after returning to Calabar, Mary's adopted daughter Janie was married to a young man who had been one of Mary's brightest students. The marriage, however, became unstable after the couple's first baby died. Janie's husband blamed himself for the death, telling himself that it had happened because he had dared to marry a twin. He left Janie, who returned to live with Mary. Mary welcomed Janie back and was doubly glad for the extra help. She had developed rheumatism, a crippling disease, which when added to her frequent bouts of malaria meant she was often unable to care for the many babies and small children that were brought to her for protection. She had many little wooden boxes that were used as cribs, and even in her sickest moments, Mary would lie in bed rocking the boxes from side to side to comfort the babies. Sadly, most of the babies died. They were usually quite sick before being sent to Mary's hut. Nevertheless, Mary and Janie took care of them. Mary believed it was important to show the Africans that every single life—even the life of a tiny baby with little hope of survival—was important to God.

Also in December 1899, a series of events began that would eventually open the way for Mary to work among the Aro people. The Aro were a shrewd people who had used witchcraft to become the strongest and most feared tribe in their area. None of the Europeans knew exactly how this witchcraft worked, at least not until Christmas 1899.

That Christmas a group of one hundred sick and dying Africans dragged themselves into a British army outpost and collapsed. The story they told was chilling. Eight hundred of them—men, women and children—had gone to the town of Arochuku on a religious pilgrimage. The Aro had convinced them that a great and wise witch doctor lived there. However, it was a trap, and the pilgrims were attacked when they arrived. Some were taken to be cooked and eaten, though most were sold as slaves to tribes farther inland. The group of one hundred people had barely managed to escape to tell the story.

When British troops heard the story, they were outraged and sent news of the incident back to military headquarters in London. It was eventually decided that Great Britain should use force to show the Aro they could no longer do such things. In August 1901, one hundred fifty British officers and several thousand African troops gathered in Duke Town for an attack on the Aro. Mary got to see them before they left because all missionaries in the area had been ordered to return to Duke Town. The British government was worried the Aro might kidnap missionaries in remote areas and use them as hostages.

Mary was not at all happy about being ripped away from "her" people, but for once she could do nothing about it.

Finally, in November the troops marched into the interior. Hundreds of people on both sides were killed, and after many days of fighting, the few surviving Aro tribesmen surrendered. However, this did not mean that peace was restored to the region. The Aro had been the controlling force in the area for so long that their defeat created chaos. Various other tribes began fighting each other for the top position of power. All Europeans were banned from entering the area except British vice-consul Sir Ralph Moore and his troops. Mary worried and prayed about what would happen to the Aro people, whom she wanted desperately to reach with the gospel message and show a better way to live.

In the meantime, Janet Wright arrived in Calabar to help Mary. Janet was one of two young girls Mary had spoken to at Falkirk during her first furlough. She had asked Mary to write to her, which Mary did, and now Janet had decided to become a missionary herself. Mary had great confidence that Janet would make a wonderful helper. Janet was particularly adept at learning the Efik and Bantu languages and was soon speaking them both well.

Mary had to wait until June 1903 to finally become involved with the Aro. She was traveling upriver from Duke Town to Akpap, and one of the passengers traveling with her was Colonel Montanaro, the commander of the raid on the Aro. The colonel was on his way back upriver to Aro territory. He and Mary struck up a conversation, and he soon told her that the British troops could not stop the fighting in the area. Before they had reached the beach near Akpap, Colonel Montanaro had a stunning idea. He begged Mary to continue upriver with him so that she could speak with the Aro chiefs. Of course, she agreed without a moment's hesitation. This was the opportunity she had prayed for.

Sure enough, Colonel Montanaro's confidence in Mary was well placed. Mary was able to get the various sides to agree on a peace treaty, and before leaving several days later, she had an open invitation to return and set up a school to teach the Aros "Book."

Mary knew she must act quickly on the invitation. The raid on the Aro had broken the spirits of the inland tribes, and for the first time, the British were now able to press inland with no resistance. They planned to build roads, bridges, canals, and docks throughout the region. Mary felt she had to reach the inland tribes with the gospel message before the area was overrun with soldiers, government officials, and traders.

In July 1904, with special permission from the British government, Mary began the first survey of the inland tribes of Calabar. Soon afterwards, Janet Wright, who was carrying on the work at Akpap, became ill and had to return to Scotland. She was replaced by two new women missionaries recently arrived from Scotland. These two women had difficulty adjusting to the situation and wrote back to Scotland complaining that no one could live under such difficult conditions: rats ran around the rafters of the mission house; it was impossible to get a good night's sleep; the food was monotonous and tasteless; the list went on and on. As a result, the two missionaries were recalled to Duke Town, and the station at Akpap was declared "too primitive" to man. Of course, everyone knew that Mary Slessor had thrived there, but by now the missions board had concluded that Mary could thrive where other missionaries could not even survive. Mary was one of a kind!

For the next ten years, Mary, aided by her daughter Janie, worked among the inland tribes. The two women conducted Bible studies, treated the sick, negotiated to stop the fighting among tribes, and saved the lives of twins. Mary also spoke out about the treatment of women and slaves. Anyone else would have been killed for challenging tribal customs and the authority of the chiefs in the way she did. But there was something different about Mary—a lone white woman carrying no gun and with no escort. Mary walked in bare feet and wore a simple dress and no hat. Wherever she went, she sang and talked of peace. She spoke the inland languages as well as the natives, and she taught people to read and write. It was as if she had been sent to help the tribes during this difficult time.

The wheels of the Foreign Missions Board in Scotland moved slowly, and Mary was always several steps ahead of it. However, the board did take her work and recommendations seriously. When Mary recommended that a place called Itu would be a good site for a mission hospital, the board agreed with her. One of Mary's longtime friends from Edinburgh donated money to build the hospital, which, much to Mary's dismay, was called the Mary Slessor Mission Hospital.

No sooner had Mary adjusted to the idea of having a hospital named after her than the British high commissioner asked her to take on the newly created role in the region of vice-consul of the native court. This meant that once again Mary would be helping to resolve disputes and stop the fighting. Despite the fact that Mary was getting older and her health was worsening with each passing year, the high commissioner convinced her that she was once again the only "man" for the job. Mary agreed to take on the position, fearing what would happen if she did not and someone with no understanding of local customs was sent into the region instead.

As promised, the British began constructing roads across the area. With the roads came a new opportunity for Mary, who discovered that she could cover much greater distances each day by riding a bicycle. Mary had a bicycle sent to her from Scotland, and soon she was whizzing up and down the new roads through the region. However, Mary's health continued to worsen, and soon, instead of pedaling a bicycle, she was being pushed around in a cart.

In 1908, one of Mary's supporters in Scotland sent her fifty pounds with the instruction that she spend it on herself. Mary wrote back, "Dear Friend, I need nothing. My every want is met and supplied without my asking." What the woman in Scotland had no way of knowing was that Mary Slessor had virtually no material possessions, nor did she want any. Mary worried over spending money on a new Bible for herself, preferring to give every penny she received to help run the churches and schools she had started.

In the early morning hours of January 13, 1915, Mary lay gravely ill in a tiny mud hut in the village of Use. She had been ill so many times before, but this time it was different. Mary knew she was dying, and so did Janie and the other children who gathered around her to keep her company. As the night wore on, Mary kept tossing her blanket off and struggling for breath. Then, in the early hours of the morning, she awoke and was offered a drink of water, which she refused. Instead, she spoke her last words. In Efik she said, "O Abassi, sana mi yok." She was asking God to release her from her pain. He did. A few minutes later Mary died.

As a rooster crowed while the early morning sun crept over the horizon, the drummers at Use beat out the sad news. Eka Kpukpru Owo—the Mother of Us All is dead. The news reverberated around the region as successive drummers drummed the news on to the next village.

The following day, a beautiful mahogany coffin was sent upriver from Duke Town, and the body of sixty-seven-year-old Mary Slessor was laid in it and carried downriver one final time.

There was not a person in Duke Town who did not know of Mary's death. In Mary's honor, all government buildings and schools were closed, flags were lowered to half-mast, and police lined the road from the dock to the mission house. Mary's funeral service was packed with people from the three tribal regions of Calabar—people to whom Mary had given thirty-nine years of her life in reaching them with the gospel message. The fact they could all gather together in one place without attacking and killing each other was perhaps the greatest tribute to Mary Slessor's work in the region. Mary's body was laid to rest in a grave on the mission compound beside those of the Reverend and Mrs. Anderson.

The United Presbyterian Church of Scotland sent out a huge slab of Scottish granite to mark Mary's grave. When Charles Ovens, Mary's carpenter friend, heard about the slab of rock, he said with a smile, "It will take more than that to keep the Mary Slessor I knew down!" In many ways he was right. Mary's example of missionary work and her willingness to sacrifice everything to reach others with the gospel message is a shining example to every Christian who desires to leave his or her homeland to do the same.

Four single Scottish women along with Janie carried on the work Mary had begun in the interior of Calabar. Five of them together found it difficult to match the workload of one petite, red-haired millworker from Dundee.

Bibliography

Buchan, James. *The Expendable Mary Slessor.* Seabury Press, 1981.

Christian, Carol, and Plummer, Gladys. *God and One Redhead: Mary Slessor of Calabar.* Hodder and Stoughton, 1970.

Enock, E. Esther. *The Missionary Heroine of Calabar: A Story of Mary Slessor.* Pickering & Inglis, Ltd., 1937.

Livingstone, W. P. *Mary Slessor of Calabar.* Zondervan Publishing House, 1984.

Miller, Basil. *Mary Slessor: Heroine of Calabar.* Bethany House Publishers, 1974.

Syme, Ronald. *The Story of Mary Slessor: Nigerian Pioneer.* William Morrow & Co., 1964.

Wellman, Sam. *Mary Slessor: Queen of Calabar.* Barbour Publishing, Inc., 1998.

About the Authors

Janet and Geoff Benge are a husband and wife writing team with more than thirty years of writing experience. Janet is a former elementary school teacher. Geoff holds a degree in history. Originally from New Zealand, the Benges spent ten years serving with Youth With A Mission. They have two daughters, Laura and Shannon, and an adopted son, Lito. They make their home in the Orlando, Florida, area.

Also from Janet and Geoff Benge...

More adventure-filled biographies for ages 10 to 100!

Christian Heroes: Then and Now

Gladys Aylward: The Adventure of a Lifetime • *978-1-57658-019-6*
Nate Saint: On a Wing and a Prayer • *978-1-57658-017-2*
Hudson Taylor: Deep in the Heart of China • *978-1-57658-016-5*
Amy Carmichael: Rescuer of Precious Gems • *978-1-57658-018-9*
Eric Liddell: Something Greater Than Gold • *978-1-57658-137-7*
Corrie ten Boom: Keeper of the Angels' Den • *978-1-57658-136-0*
William Carey: Obliged to Go • *978-1-57658-147-6*
George Müller: Guardian of Bristol's Orphans • *978-1-57658-145-2*
Jim Elliot: One Great Purpose • *978-1-57658-146-9*
Mary Slessor: Forward into Calabar • *978-1-57658-148-3*
David Livingstone: Africa's Trailblazer • *978-1-57658-153-7*
Betty Greene: Wings to Serve • *978-1-57658-152-0*
Adoniram Judson: Bound for Burma • *978-1-57658-161-2*
Cameron Townsend: Good News in Every Language • *978-1-57658-164-3*
Jonathan Goforth: An Open Door in China • *978-1-57658-174-2*
Lottie Moon: Giving Her All for China • *978-1-57658-188-9*
John Williams: Messenger of Peace • *978-1-57658-256-5*
William Booth: Soup, Soap, and Salvation • *978-1-57658-258-9*
Rowland Bingham: Into Africa's Interior • *978-1-57658-282-4*
Ida Scudder: Healing Bodies, Touching Hearts • *978-1-57658-285-5*
Wilfred Grenfell: Fisher of Men • *978-1-57658-292-3*
Lillian Trasher: The Greatest Wonder in Egypt • *978-1-57658-305-0*
Loren Cunningham: Into All the World • *978-1-57658-199-5*
Florence Young: Mission Accomplished • *978-1-57658-313-5*
Sundar Singh: Footprints Over the Mountains • *978-1-57658-318-0*
C.T. Studd: No Retreat • *978-1-57658-288-6*
Rachel Saint: A Star in the Jungle • *978-1-57658-337-1*
Brother Andrew: God's Secret Agent • *978-1-57658-355-5*
Clarence Jones: Mr. Radio • *978-1-57658-343-2*
Count Zinzendorf: Firstfruit • *978-1-57658-262-6*
John Wesley: The World His Parish • *978-1-57658-382-1*
C. S. Lewis: Master Storyteller • *978-1-57658-385-2*
David Bussau: Facing the World Head-on • *978-1-57658-415-6*
Jacob DeShazer: Forgive Your Enemies • *978-1-57658-475-0*
Isobel Kuhn: On the Roof of the World • *978-1-57658-497-2*
Elisabeth Elliot: Joyful Surrender • *978-1-57658-513-9*

D. L. Moody: Bringing Souls to Christ • 978-1-57658-552-8
Paul Brand: Helping Hands • 978-1-57658-536-8
Dietrich Bonhoeffer: In the Midst of Wickedness • 978-1-57658-713-3
Francis Asbury: Circuit Rider • 978-1-57658-737-9
Samuel Zwemer: The Burden of Arabia • 978-1-57658-738-6
Klaus-Dieter John: Hope in the Land of the Incas • 978-1-57658-826-2
Mildred Cable: Through the Jade Gate • 978-1-57658-886-4
John Flynn: Into the Never Never • 978-1-57658-898-7

Heroes of History

George Washington Carver: From Slave to Scientist • 978-1-883002-78-7
Abraham Lincoln: A New Birth of Freedom • 978-1-883002-79-4
Meriwether Lewis: Off the Edge of the Map • 978-1-883002-80-0
George Washington: True Patriot • 978-1-883002-81-7
William Penn: Liberty and Justice for All • 978-1-883002-82-4
Harriet Tubman: Freedombound • 978-1-883002-90-9
John Adams: Independence Forever • 978-1-883002-50-3
Clara Barton: Courage under Fire • 978-1-883002-51-0
Daniel Boone: Frontiersman • 978-1-932096-09-5
Theodore Roosevelt: An American Original • 978-1-932096-10-1
Douglas MacArthur: What Greater Honor • 978-1-932096-15-6
Benjamin Franklin: Live Wire • 978-1-932096-14-9
Christopher Columbus: Across the Ocean Sea • 978-1-932096-23-1
Laura Ingalls Wilder: A Storybook Life • 978-1-932096-32-3
Orville Wright: The Flyer • 978-1-932096-34-7
John Smith: A Foothold in the New World • 978-1-932096-36-1
Thomas Edison: Inspiration and Hard Work • 978-1-932096-37-8
Alan Shepard: Higher and Faster • 978-1-932096-41-5
Ronald Reagan: Destiny at His Side • 978-1-932096-65-1
Milton Hershey: More Than Chocolate • 978-1-932096-82-8
Billy Graham: America's Pastor • 978-1-62486-024-9
Ben Carson: A Chance at Life • 978-1-62486-034-8
Louis Zamperini: Redemption • 978-1-62486-049-2
Elizabeth Fry: Angel of Newgate • 978-1-62486-064-5
William Wilberforce: Take Up the Fight • 978-1-62486-057-7
William Bradford: Plymouth's Rock • 978-1-62486-092-8